Write the Vision:
HOW TO DEVELOP
A LIFE PLAN

Kyle Searcy

Published by

KCS MINISTRIES
6000 Monticello Dr
Montgomery, AL 36116

Unless otherwise indicated, all Scripture quotations are taken from the New *King James Bible.*

Write the Vision

ISBN 978-1-64764-067-5
Copyright 2022 by Kyle Searcy

Published by

KCS Ministries
6000 Monticello Dr
Montgomery, AL 36116
334-613-3363

ACKNOWLEDGMENTS

To all those with dreams deferred, do not let them dry up like a raisin in the sun. Fulfill them. Maximize your potential. Be all that God has created you to be.

Suggestion:

To all those who have had their dreams put off, don't let them dry out in the sun like a raisin. They must be met. Make the most of your abilities. Be everything God intended for you to be.

CONTENTS

PART 1
FOUNDATIONS OF VISION

Chapter 1

THE IMPORTANCE OF PLANNING

*"I will stand upon my watch, and set me upon the tower, and will
watch to see what he will say unto me, and what I shall answer
when I am reproved. And the Lord answered me, and said,
Write the vision, and make it plain."
(AMP) Habakkuk 2:1-2.*

A while ago, my wife and I were tired and needed a break for a few days. We just needed a change of environment. So, I called her and said, "Pack our clothes and let's go away for a few days." When we got into the car, she asked where we were going. I pointed in front of us and said, in a light, fun way, "this way." She smiled, and literally, we went "that way." We traveled out of Montgomery on Highway 65 and passed through Birmingham. I had not planned a thing; I just decided that we would get in the car and travel until we were tired. We drove for miles before finally deciding to find a place to sleep.

The first small town that we arrived at did not have any hotel vacancies, so we continued to drive until we finally got to a little town in Tennessee called Hendersonville, where a TBN facility is located. We stopped and decided to see what TBN had scheduled for the evening. To our surprise, they were featuring an opera. You may think opera is great, but I don't like opera. We sat through it anyway, but I didn't enjoy it. My choice of music is something with a little more thump and excitement than what an opera can offer.

Later, we found a hotel with a vacancy and went to sleep. When our adventure was over, had indeed rested, but our little vacation could have been much better if we had created a plan. I learned from that experience that if you don't know where you're going, any road can take you there. When you do get "there," you may not even know where you are because you had no idea where you were going when you started.

Habakkuk understood this principle. In the first chapter of his book, Habakkuk looked at the circumstances around him and saw that a wicked army, the Chaldeans, was oppressing righteous Israel. Habakkuk was so concerned about the situation that he asked God, "God, what can I do?" He purposed in his heart that he would stand upon his watch, listen to God, talk to Him, and wait for an answer. God's answer to Habakkuk was to "write the vision and make it plain so that the person who read the vision could run with it." In other words, God was telling Habakkuk that He had a plan for dealing with the Chaldeans, and He wanted Habakkuk to write that plan so that everyone would know and understand God's course of action.

God's directions to Habakkuk still have relevance today. The command to have a vision and write it down keeps you from relegating your life to the game of "chance." What you want to accomplish personally, professionally, domestically, and spiritually in your life will not be the result of chance; it will be the result of a vision. Chance has almost nothing to do with what you will become, but vision has everything to do with your future.

MENTAL SIGHT

What is a vision? A Vision is a clear mental picture of what you have in mind to achieve. Vision is different from *hope*; vision is *sight*. A vision is so real to you that you can see it in your mind's eye. It is a modification of conditions that do not currently exist. People think in pictures as opposed to words. If I tell you to think about an elephant, you will not see the word "e-l-e-p-h-a-n-t." Instead, you will see a giant grey creature with a trunk. If I tell you to think about a tree, you will not see the word "t-r-e-e." You will see the mental picture of how a tree looks.

Therefore, the vision for your life is not "hope"; neither is it a list nor a wish. It is a clear mental picture of what you want to be in life. It's a clear picture in your mind's eye of your destiny. Before I formed thee in the belly, I knew thee." (Jeremiah 1:5) Vision sees the future before it comes to be.

In essence, a vision is a clear mental image of a preferable future imparted by God to his servants which is based on an accurate understanding of God, self, and circumstances. In your mind's eye , you are given a portrait of what could be better, not maintaining the status quo. It is always future-focused and does not try to replicate the past. A vision is always imparted by God as He desires to build His kingdom. It is not about relying on our

13

talents, abilities, and experience. He may use these, but His vision is built beyond what we can humanly do.

Vision isn't about you or me. It's all about God, and His purposes are unique to you and me. Vision emanates from purpose. Vision is given to individuals, and because it is God-given, vision is greater than the visionary who receives it. God's purposes for mankind are clear. God's vision can often include multiple generations. It will leave a legacy that lasts well beyond the individual who received it. For example, David received the vision of the building, and his son, Solomon, fulfilled the vision in brick and mortar.

Vision is most often manifested in phases. Looking at David's life, we first see his anointing in Bethlehem when Samuel chose him to be the next king. He had a vision of what being king should and should not be as he observed Saul and his commanders. In the cave of Adullam, David learned how the vision could only be achieved through humility and honor. He learned how vision is in God's timing and not man's. While in Judah, David was crowned king. Yet that was not the total fulfillment of God's vision for the king's life. He had a vision of Zion, the place of the Lord in Jerusalem, with a temple built for God's glory and the people's worship. Each step advanced the vision forward, even though it might have looked like circumstances were pushing it backward. The lessons we learn in the process will bring the vision to fulfillment.

In many cases, visions don't come fully formed; they unfold within the scope of the time that they meant for. Even if people do have a vision, it is not usually clear enough. It should be so clear that you can write it in intricate detail. Most people don't receive it very clearly, so they can "make it plain" when talking to others.

What is a vision? Here are some quotes that summarize its characteristics. Vision is:

"Foresight with insight based on hindsight;"

"Seeing the invisible and making it visible;"

"Information that bridges the present to the future;"

"Sanctified dreams."

THE POWER OF THE PEN

Even though vision is sight, there is awesome power in the pen. The great church reformer Martin Luther once said, "*The faintest ink is better than the sharpest memory.*" In God's admonishment to Habakkuk, if we are to accomplish our purpose in life, we must not limit our vision to mental "sight" alone. We must learn to write our vision down so that when we read it, we actually feel like running. Being able to read what we have "seen or created" mentally (in our minds) helps us during times of discouragement. Writing helps us focus our attention. Remember, "A man's heart plans his way, but the Lord directs his steps." (Proverbs 16:9)

Michael LeBoeuf said, "*When you write down your ideas, you automatically focus your attention on them. Few, if any, of us can write one thought and think another at the same time. Thus, a pencil and paper make excellent concentration tools.*" People who write their goals down are 39.5% more likely to succeed. People who write their goals and share their progress with people that they've chosen to hold them accountable are 76.7% more likely to achieve them. Your success is increased just by writing. Writing is vital to a phenomenon called, "**Encoding.**"

Encoding is what happens in the brain when we encounter an event, thought, knowledge, etc., and that information is transferred to the hippocampus to be analyzed. The hippocampus has the wonderful task of deciding what to store in our long-term memory and what to purge.

When a thought is written down in your own words, your mind attaches greater importance to it, causing the thought to be stored more prominently and be remembered. Neuropsychologists call this the "generation effect." 1 As powerful as this phenomenon is, we still have approximately 97% of the population that does not have clearly defined written goals. I hope to change that number with this book.

If you have not written down your vision before now, do not despair. Before you finish this book, I believe that God will not only give you a vision (or a more focused vision), but you will also be able to write your life plan clearly and concisely. You will have a plan, you will have a life goal, and you will understand the steps you need to take to get to your goal. There is great power in a written plan. God does not operate by sheer spontaneity. As Christians, we somehow have the idea that because we have an omnipresent, omniscient, and almighty God, He is going to do everything for us. He is not. Instead, God waits to see us take action towards actualizing the vision. The steps or actions are what God anoints for our success. He promised to bless our hands; actions not just our minds; thoughts. For success, we have to commit our steps or actions to Him. Psalm 37:5 says, *"Commit thy way unto the Lord; trust also in him, and he shall bring it to pass."*

Action is as important as having a vision and writing it down. Vision is not enough; it can only be accomplished when actions are taken. It is God's duty to give a vision, but your duty to take action to get it actualized. When you take the necessary steps to realize your vision, God will bless and bring it to fruition.

LITTLE BECOMES MUCH

Matthew 14:13-21 gives us a clear example of how God will bless what we give Him, no matter how small it is. When Jesus was teaching the multitudes, they became hungry. The disciples came, saying, "Jesus, send the people away; they are hungry." But Jesus said, "Give them something to eat." The disciples were only able to find two fish and five loaves of bread, a meal prepared for one small child. The disciples could not see the greatness in what they had to offer. But Jesus said, "Bring what you have." Jesus took their small offering, blessed it, multiplied it, and fed more than five thousand people with it. God takes what you have, anoints it, and uses it. Many times, we say we are waiting on God. Nevertheless, God is waiting on us. He is waiting for us to realize what we can do and who we can be.

We have a major responsibility in securing our destiny. This principle is visible in Jesus' dealings with those whose lives He touched. For example, as Jesus walked the streets of Galilee, one day He encountered a blind man who said, "Jesus, have mercy on me." Jesus asked him a question: "What do you want me to do for you?" Now, it was obvious that the man was blind and apparently wanted Jesus to heal him; but Jesus wanted something from the man. Jesus wanted to know what this man needed and whether he believed Jesus was able to perform a miracle in his life. In other words, Jesus was pointing out that the blind man had a responsibility for the performance of a miracle that was part of his destiny. The same is true for Christians today. In everything God does for us, there is both God's responsibility and ours. God's sovereignty is at work, but human responsibility must come to bear as well. As Christians, we can do nothing without God, but God will often do nothing without us. He expects us to bring something to the table before He moves in our lives.

This means that where you end up ten years from now should not be accidental; it should be purposeful. You must have a clearly defined vision to ensure that you are able to help determine where your life is going.

THE VALUE OF VISION

Why is vision so important? Many benefits are obvious; however, some may have eluded you. Compare each of these with your life currently.

❖ **Vision keeps you on a specific path.**

Daily distractions too often make us lose focus. Vision, however, gives us a myopic spotlight that keeps us treading in the right direction no matter what pulls our attention away from our goals. What kept Abraham Lincoln going after so many setbacks on his way to becoming President? It was the vision. Perhaps I would have quit after the thirtieth try and decided to invent cookies or something. But the vision, the thought or picture firmly planted in Lincoln's mind's eye, kept him on a specific path. Today, all of us have him to thank for changing our nation for the better.

❖ **Vision encourages you toward performance**.

Most people's life productivity is cut almost in half by the absence of vision. King Solomon, the wisest king to ever live, teaches us that no vision equals no discipline.

> Proverbs 29:18
> "Where *there is* no revelation, the people cast off restraint;
> But happy *is* he who keeps the law."

Without vision, your energy and resources remain scattered rather than finding a channel toward a worthwhile objective. Not having a goal means you won't take steps toward accomplishing one. A life that aims at nothing on a daily basis will almost certainly hit its target – nothing. The life that daily aims at the desired vision will also surely hit that goal.

❖ **Vision gives significance to the details of your life.**

Vision causes us to see the benefits of the seemingly mundane or tedious tasks in our lives. As a former math teacher, I was often asked by students why they needed to take algebra. They could not see how learning complicated formulas would help them later in life. My answer was that they should not focus on the need for algebra itself, but rather see the class as one of many stepping-stones to their future. The ability to reason in formulas is something that can help in multiple careers that aren't directly related to math. But in order to see algebra's worth, though, they needed to have a vision for their lives. The same is true for Christians. Once we have a vision of the larger picture, we are better able to deal with the steps that God has ordered to bring us to our "expected end."

❖ **Vision brings passion.**

Vision evokes emotion. If you have a clear vision, you should become emotional just thinking about it. Having a vision is similar to the "coming attractions" at the beginning of a movie. The coming attractions give you a preview of a movie that is not in the theaters yet. The idea is to get you excited about what is yet to come. That is the way vision works. A vision is a mental picture of what will exist in your future. You could be in a bad situation today, but having a vision brings you the joy of knowing you are not destined to stay where you are. Sometimes you have to "see" yourself delivered from your present circumstances. Then you must speak to your destiny. Say to yourself, "I may be broke, busted, and disgusted today, but I will be rich, prosperous, and giving to the kingdom in just a little while because I know my vision." Understanding the awesome nature of your vision allows you to experience emotions that are associated with an anticipated future.

❖ **Vision motivates to endure hardships.**

I remember a vision I developed when I was younger. I grew up in New York in what can be described as a "bad" neighborhood. There were some housing projects down the street, and the people who lived there traveled in packs of nine or ten. Often, when Mama sent me to the store to get some bread and milk, they would meet me coming out of the store and rob me. Since I could not win in a fight against nine or ten people, whatever they wanted, they took it.

I finally got tired of it and decided I had to do something. I decided to learn martial arts. Learning martial arts was extremely difficult. It required discipline and demanding physical activity, but I was one of the best in my class because I was very motivated by my "vision" to stand up against my tormentors. While doing pushups on my knuckles, I would visualize the day when the bullies would come to try to rob me, and I would be able to handle all of them. I was motivated by the vision of becoming a modern-day Bruce Lee. My vision motivated me to endure whatever I had to go through because of what I "saw" in my future. Vision helps you to endure life's hardships because you know that your "change is coming."

❖ **Vision provides direction.**

It is your mental roadmap. Vision sets boundaries in your life. A former member of the church I pastor was very aware of the need for boundaries in his life. As a professional boxer, his daily routine was dominated by boundaries. He was up by six every morning. He would run for five miles, eat a big breakfast, and take a nap. Later, he would go to the gym and work out for several hours. This was his daily routine. He observed the boundaries in his life because he wanted to win. His vision caused him to be "restrained." Proverbs 29:18 says, "*Where there is no vision, the people perish.*" The word *perish* means "to cast off restraint." If you do not have a vision, you have nothing to restrain you, nothing to hold you within boundaries. You do not have any dos and don'ts, so anything goes. When anything goes, everything will go. As a result, you must have the vision to give you direction.

❖ **Vision gives purpose.**

When you really understand the vision, your self-worth increases. Suddenly, *you* matter because you now have a vision of accomplishing something that only you can do. Your vision is something God ordained for you to do, and only *you* can do it. Having a vision causes your self-esteem to rise because you know that you have value, and you know that the earth will miss something if you are not on it. Just as nobody else has your fingerprints, nobody else has your God-given vision. That is why it is so important that you find your vision.

Zig Ziglar the great salesman and motivational speaker once said "You must have goals in your life. You must become a "meaningful specific" rather than a "wandering generality."

PREPARING FOR YOUR LIFE PLAN

Here are some questions for you to begin discovering your vision and its component goals. Give thought to these so that you can refer to them later.

Have you ever had a specific plan for a long-term goal and worked until the goal was fulfilled? Then answer the following:

1. How did you determine the goal? What resources did you use?

_____

_____

_____

_____

2. How did the goal help you make choices to keep you on the path to fulfillment?

_____

_____

_____

_____

3. Did you receive encouragement as you worked toward the goal's fulfillment?

_____

_____

_____

_____

4. Did you begin to see small details of your life in light of the goal ahead?

_____

_____

_____

_____

5. Did your goal excite and motivate you? In what ways?

_____

_____

_____

_____

6. Did you encounter hardships on the pathway to your goal? How were you able to deal with these?

_____

_____

_____

_____

7. When making choices about your goal, did you know the direction you had to go?

_____

_____

_____

_____

8. Did you feel purpose in your life as you participated in the journey toward your goal?

_____

_____

_____

_____

If you have never had any vision or goal in your life, answer the following:

1. Why do you think you have never had a vision in your life?

_____

_____

_____

_____

2. Is it difficult for you to think of the future and a plan to secure that future? Why or why not?

_____

_____

_____

_____

3. Have you ever felt you were wandering aimlessly through life without a purpose?

_____

_____

_____

_____

4. Have you wanted to be more goal-oriented and find a path to a preferred future? Why or why not?

_____

_____

_____

_____

5. Would you be willing to spend time with God to asking and determining your vision? Why or why not?

_____

_____

_____

_____

Chapter 2

HOW TO FIND VISION

Many people have ideas. But their ideas are not visions. Other people have dreams, but dreams are not the same as visions. How do you distinguish your dreams and ideas from God's vision? Once you have a dream or a vision, what are you supposed to do? The Bible says, "Make your calling and election sure." So, God expects us to *know* what He wants us to do. More specifically, the verse (2 Peter 1:10) says, *"Make diligence to make your calling and election sure."* Some versions use the word *"strive"* for "make diligence." So, how do you show diligence or strive toward your vision? More importantly, how do you even determine what it is and what your vision is not?

A vision does not always come from some angelic revelation. Sometimes we get so spiritually "spooky" that we say we do not know what to do because the Lord has not "revealed it to us" yet. Finding a vision is not done by willpower or a chance set of supernatural experiences. How is it found?

My friend Chris had a meeting with the Ministry Director over a volunteer celebration they were to have. Chris had some powerful ideas for how to celebrate and worship God while thanking the workers. The Ministry Director only heard Chris' words, "I have some ideas," and interrupted by saying, "Chris, that's the problem. You always have ideas." Chris was offended by the remark, but later realized the Ministry Director wanted a vision for the event, not just ideas.

REQUIREMENTS TO DISCOVER VISION:

It is important to separate our own ideas from God-given visions. But first, we must critically examine if we are ready to perceive God's vision within our lives. We can easily prepare ourselves by meeting four requirements.

1. Comprehending God: You should have a basic understanding of what God wants you to do. This does not need to be specific or comprehensive at this point, but easy to picture. If you are at ease comprehending God's direction in your life, you will be able to hear His vision in your spiritual ear.

2. Knowing Yourself: You need to know your own abilities, gifts, limitations, values, and desires before you can truly seek His vision for your life. Vision does not promote your own desires, even if they are beneficial to others. Vision incorporates our abilities within the greater plan of God.

3. Truly Understanding Circumstances: God is not going to wave His hand and align all circumstances to make an easy path to the fulfillment of His vision. Instead, the journey toward the vision is just as important as the end goal. Circumstances may bring detours; some may almost destroy our pathway. However, these events and circumstances cannot limit our potential. Putting current and changing

circumstances into proper perspective helps us create a realistic pathway to receive the vision from beginning to end.

4. Being a Humble Visionary: It is not your responsibility to make up a vision. It is not your responsibility to make sure you reach your goal. It is not your victory or defeat at the goal's end. Ultimately, the vision is the Lord's. Continue to let Him be in charge while you remain teachable and obedient. And the ultimate goal of the vision is to glorify God!

DISCOVERING A VISION:

To receive a vision, the stage must be set with the understanding that either something is missing or something could be improved. The impetus for vision includes the inability to accept things the way they are. This dissatisfaction with present circumstances or conditions grows when you know that you can help make them better. The vision may grow as *something* inside you recognizes the need to change or rise to a new level. You begin to realize, "I can't stay like this; I'm not going to live like this. I can do better than this. I can *be* better than this. I can look better than this. I can even *smell* better than this." That is a beginning, but that is not yet a vision. Many people may see that things are not as they should be, but it takes more than "seeing" to make things right. The mental picture is the first step, but it is still not a vision. If you want a vision, you must go beyond that picture. You have to get to a place where you have a strong conviction that something should be done to correct whatever is wrong.

Vision development is a three-step process: (1) Dissatisfaction or acknowledgment that something could be better, (2) Mental image, and (3) Conviction. Here's an example: **Dissatisfaction:** "I'm so tired of being broke. I don't know what to do." **Mental Image:** "I see myself grocery shopping without worrying about the bank account. But if you stop here, you are still dreaming. You must go on to the next step. **Conviction:** "I have to develop a plan to help me realize my dream." Without the conviction or burden to change the circumstances around you, you might end up being just a dreamer rather than a visionary. Many people have dreams or wishes, but dreams and wishes are not visions. A vision comes when there is a conviction, an imperative, or a demand that will not let you rest. It is a fire burning in your spiritual bones that compels you to do something about whatever situation needs to be changed. That "fire" is the real vision that motivates you to action.

THE CONCEPTION OF VISION:

How is a vision conceived? Vision begins as a concern and develops into a burden. Habakkuk was burdened when he saw the Chaldeans coming against his people. His burden moved him to action. Another biblical example of a burden leading to action is found in the book of Nehemiah. Nehemiah was so troubled by the condition of the children of Israel that the Bible says he sat down and mourned and wept for several days. Then he did something. He rebuilt the walls of Jerusalem. (More about this later.) Now, you have to ask yourself some questions. What burdens you in life? What troubles you? A God-given vision is always focused on others. Even your personal vision is always going to have something to do with others. Do you realize that most great men achieved their success without seeking to be great? Martin Luther King did not say, "I have a dream that one day I'll win a Nobel Peace Prize, or one day there will be streets all over the country named after me." Dr. King's vision was focused on his conviction to bring about a better day for all people. By following his vision, Dr. King achieved fame and success. His life followed a Biblical principle: *"Seek ye first the kingdom of God, and His righteousness, and all other things will be added unto you."* (Matthew 6:33)

Your vision is going to be bigger than just you and your situation. Vision cannot focus on acquiring things. Your vision must be connected to doing something good for humanity. Again, a vision that is truly inspired by God will always be focused on others. It is always going to have to do with helping somebody else. Even the one who says his vision is to be a businessman has to realize that his vision must be focused on meeting the needs of others. A successful businessman sees a need and meets it. Sam Walton saw a need and met it through a business called Wal-Mart. His children are still reaping the benefits of their father's vision. Likewise, your vision has to provide a service, and the by-product of that service will be prosperity, so **those whose focus is only on riches will end up falling into snares and many hurtful and foolish lusts.** We will look closer at this issue and others later in the book.

Your vision should not be to just get rich. Riches come when you find your niche, when you find your place, and when you find your vision. When you find what God has ordained for you to do and you do it with joy, money is the by-product. The motivation behind your vision cannot be selfish. Your vision cannot be "my-focused" or "me-focused"; it has to be others-focused. You must ask yourself why God placed you on Earth. What is your purpose in the lives of others? What are you supposed to do to make someone else's life better? Are you supposed to teach children or just raise your own children? Are you supposed to have a business? There is some need in humanity that you are supposed to meet. When you are "about your Heavenly Father's business," you will find true joy.

MY BURDEN:

We have established that vision begins with a burden, "something" inside of you that you just cannot shake. You find yourself daydreaming about it; it is constantly on your mind. I know my vision. I know what I am supposed to do in life because I know what I have daydreamed about for years. My vision is to be a worshiper of God and a deliverer of men. I want to worship God and see men delivered all around the world. When I "daydream," I imagine that I am laying hands on blind people and their eyes are opening. I see myself being used by God to help heal others of cancer or to help couples restore their marriages. Those are some of my dreams. I know what God has put in me. It is a burden, and it is something that I have to do. People need to be free; they need to find God. That is my burden. I can't shake it; I can't get it off of me. My prayer is, "God, you've got to give me more power because I'm burdened. I have to see people set free!" What burns in you? What touches you? What deeply affects you? Maybe you have not seen all of your vision yet, but *something* ought to move you. If you find what moves you, you will find the vision for your life. Something ought to bring deep, intense conviction and motivation to your heart; when you find that *thing*, you will find your true vision. We will delve deeper into discovering the burden/vision concept later.

TIMING OF THE VISION:

Even after you find your true vision, you still must wait on God's timing. Realizing your vision does not necessarily mean that you must act on it immediately. The fact that God gives you a vision today does not mean that you have to do something about it tomorrow. God may give you a vision today and say all you can do now is write it down and pray for it to manifest. It may be that you are not yet ready to handle the vision God has for your life. Moses had the vision to deliver the children of Israel. Instead of waiting for God's timing, Moses tried to make the vision come to pass by killing an Egyptian. At that point, God said, "Wait. I need to teach this boy some lessons." He sent Moses into the wilderness to be trained in the "School of Hard Knocks and Knee-ology" for forty years. After his time of preparation, God brought Moses out of the wilderness, prepared to fulfill his vision.

Every vision has its own timing, but do not use that as an excuse not to move. For many of you, the time has come. So, do not just sit back and say, "It's not time yet, so I can't do anything now." No. This book is your wake-up call. You need to wake up, shake up, and get to work on the vision God has given you. Shake the dust off and get to work for Jesus. Many of us are far too inactive. We need to get up and do something so that God can have something to bless. However, before you get started, you need a life plan. Look and listen for the preparation God needs you to do before the work begins.

PREPARING FOR YOUR LIFE PLAN

Here are some questions for you to begin discovering your vision and its component goals. Give thought to these so that you can refer to them later.

Assuming you desire to receive a vision from God, answer the following:

1. Have you ever been called to do something for your church or for a person you know?

   _____

   _____

   _____

   _____

2. How did you know you were called to do this and it wasn't just a good idea?

   _____

   _____

   _____

3. Do you understand the difference between a great idea and a vision? Have you experienced receiving a vision for your life? How was that different than any wonderful idea you have had?

   _____

   _____

   _____

   _____

4. Where are you currently in terms of the requirements for conceiving a vision? Consider each one as it personally applies to your life:

   - Comprehending God
   - Knowing Myself
   - Truly Understanding Circumstances
   - Being a Humble Visionary

   _____

   _____

   _____

   _____

5. Evaluate where you are in the three-step process.

   - Dissatisfaction
   - Mental Image
   - Conviction.

   _____

   _____

   _____

   _____

6. How are you able to keep from being "me-focused" when you are doing good for God?

   _____

   _____

   _____

   _____

Chapter 3

WHAT YOU BRING TO THE TABLE

When you develop your life plan, it helps to assess aspects of your life that you have developed thus far. This includes who you are and what you have done up until this point. Without this assessment, you can quickly get off track and plan beyond what God has already placed in you. On the flip side, you can also plan with cowardice, be afraid to go beyond what you have accomplished, and rely on God's grace to enable you in your weakness to fulfill the vision He gives to you. These two issues will help you look at your history with new eyes. You will not be held down because of the past or ignore what God has built within you.

The Bible exhorts us to enumerate our history. Isaiah 46:9 (MSG) says, *"Remember your history, your long and rich history."* For Israel, it was a way for parents to teach their children about the goodness of God. The Jews still observe festivals that celebrate their history: deliverance from Egypt (Passover), escaping evil in Persia through Esther (Purim), and others that acknowledge God's hand in their lives.

YOUR HISTORY

Your history is worth celebrating as well. One way to begin this process is to create a timeline of your life from birth to now. On the timeline, first place significant events in your life...like a special birthday, graduation, first job, marriage, first house, first child , significant deaths, etc. These are like markers for placing the rest of the information.

Next, take one of the following areas of life and follow it through the timeline.

1. Spiritual Walk
2. Family Life
3. Service to God
4. Career
5. Your Inner Self (Mental, Emotional)
6. Leisure, Hobbies, and Vacations
7. Financial Assets
8. Health

For example, if you were to begin with Spiritual Walk, you may have a date for when you first heard the Gospel, when you accepted Jesus' gift of grace, when you were filled with the Holy Spirit, when you first led someone to Christ, when you went to a significant retreat and felt the Lord's presence like never before, when you joined the church, when you first heard the call to volunteer for a ministry, and any other significant memories of a spiritual nature.

Go through each one and spend time calling to remembrance/ mind the way God has shaped you. Some of the items on the timeline may be victories, some may be achievements, some may be difficult events, some may even feel like setbacks or failures. The tapestry of your life is woven with dark threads as well as bright-colored threads. Each adds to the creation of the picture of who you currently are.

This exercise may take some time to do well. If you pray as you remember and write, ask God to give you His perspective into the nature of the event or situation. Let Him bring healing where needed, new life where something seems to have died, and rejoicing where there have been victories. Let the Holy Spirit breathe life into your history. A cloud of witnesses has been cheering you on. (Hebrews12:7) Jesus stands before the Father (Romans 8:34) on your behalf to give beauty for ashes and water in the desert places.

Believe me when I say that your timeline is a testimony. It gives witness to God's keeping power and His love toward you. That you are alive today verifies these facts. In fact, I want to encourage you to share your timeline with someone you know to allow them to hear of God's work in your life.

SPACE FOR YOUR HISTORICAL TIMELINE

PART 2
NEHEMIAH: FROM VISIONARY TO CULMINATION

Chapter 4

NEHEMIAH:
THE VISIONARY

As we work toward writing our life plan, it is prudent to look at someone who had a great history but, midway through life, needed to do an about-face as far as what he would do for God. His history came to bear on who he was in the midst of new responsibilities and their accompanying challenges. Our observations will give us clues on how to map out our future and prepare for unforeseen challenges. We can come out the other side having fulfilled God's vision for our lives!

The Bible contains an awesome story about a man named Nehemiah (See Nehemiah 1:1-11). Nehemiah lived with and served King Artaxerxes as his cupbearer. The cupbearer's position was very important. He literally protected the life of the king by tasting the king's food or drinking the king's beverage before he ate or drank. This was a means of protecting the king from being poisoned by his enemies. If an enemy was able to gain influence over the cupbearer, then the cupbearer could easily be the cause of the king's death. Because of his importance to the king's very life, the cupbearer's relationship with the king was one of great trust and intimacy.

Nehemiah enjoyed that relationship with Artaxerxes, even though Nehemiah was actually a slave. His people, the Jews, had been taken captive years before Nehemiah's appointment to the king's court. The Jews' captivity was part of their punishment for sinning against God. God allowed their enemies to destroy the Jewish temple, tear down their walls, and take the people captive to various lands. Somehow, Nehemiah made it into the king's palace in Shushan and became the king's cupbearer.

I like Nehemiah because he did not forget where he came from once he made it to a new level. He did not become complacent because he could wear royal apparel, sleep in a comfortable bed every night, and hold the king's cup. When Nehemiah learned that the walls of his homeland had not been repaired, the Bible says Nehemiah became concerned. He fasted, he mourned, and he wept for days before God. A burden began to develop in him, bringing him the conviction that he could not sit back and let his people suffer; he knew he had to do something about the conditions in his homeland. For some time, Nehemiah did nothing; then, God began to orchestrate circumstances for Nehemiah to act. Nehemiah went to the king and said, "King, I've got problems back home, and I need to do something about them." He asked the king's permission to rebuild the walls of Jerusalem. After the king granted his request, Nehemiah went back home and accomplished his goal in only fifty-two days.

Why were the walls so important? Understand that Nehemiah's time was different from our own. Walls were the only protection ancient cities had against the attacks of their enemies. They built massive walls around entire cities, with strategically positioned gates. These gates were the only way in and out of these cities. Gatekeepers were placed at each entrance to warn people of pending attacks. The walls were the cities' primary means of security. Without walls, a city did not have any protection. So, the walls of Jerusalem were vital to the survival of the Jews.

Nehemiah's concern was that his people and his hometown did not have protection, and without protection, they could not be restored as a viable society. This concern forced Nehemiah out of his "comfort zone." Nehemiah left the palace with a mindset and a vision, but with whom did he have to work? His only choice of workers was those who were broke, discouraged, discontented, and troubled. Yet, these were the ones who had to help Nehemiah accomplish a monumental task in a relatively short period of time. We know that Nehemiah did accomplish his task; but how did he do it? Nehemiah heard and understood something that we all must have, and that is "vision." When you want to study about vision in the Bible, the man to study was Nehemiah. Nehemiah developed a vision, he worked on his vision, and he saw it come to pass.

Nehemiah's desire to see Jerusalem's walls rebuilt fulfilled the characteristics of a true vision. He had a mental picture of what existed, and he was dissatisfied with the situation. He had a strong conviction that walls were necessary. His situation in Persia was one where he could have the ear of the king. Therefore, he wasn't just hopeful that someone else might come along to rebuild the walls. He was able to see circumstances aligning that gave him a clear picture of his destiny. He lived and dreamed the vision so much, he wept and was consumed by it.

Every one of us ought to have a vision for our lives. You cannot just continue to go through life *hoping* things get better, *hoping* things open up, *hoping* one day to become what you want to be. You must have a plan, a goal, or a vision for your life to give you purpose and direction. It is not enough to just end up "somewhere"; you need to end up somewhere on purpose.

PREDESTINED PURPOSE

Predestined purpose means that you should decide **now** where you are going to be tomorrow. As mentioned earlier, *"If you don't know where you're going, when you end up 'there,' you'll be somewhere, but you won't be 'there' because you won't know where 'there' is."*

A lot of people live their lives not knowing where "there" is. Have you ever run into people with a 'victim' mentality? Everything that happens to them is somebody else's fault. Their lives are based on a series of excuses: "*They* gave me an 'F'." "*They* didn't give me a job." "It's the man's fault." "I'm the wrong color." Everything is always someone else's fault. That mindset says that life happens to you; you don't make life happen. That mindset says life is like casting lots; it is a matter of chance.

On the other hand, some people work to make their vision happen. Bill Gates did not just randomly become the richest man in the world; he worked for his success. Read his biography to learn how he slept at his desk for weeks at a time, rarely going home. He did not even eat most of the time. He was trying to work on his vision and passion. Some might think Tiger Woods came out of the womb anointed to play golf. Tiger Woods worked tirelessly to perfect his craft. The same can be said of other athletes. Michael Jordan had to do more than "believe" he could fly. He worked out constantly; he was diligent in the pursuit of his purpose. Harriet Tubman didn't just hope that the slaves could escape bondage. She saw their future and pictured how she could secure freedom for over 300 people. Then she worked tirelessly to make the vision come to fruition. Many people do not understand that if you really want something, you must work to implement your plan.

A successful life does not just happen. It is a result of planning and of having goals and a vision. The problem is that most people do not have the vision. You must understand, though, that every single thing that you desire to become professionally, spiritually, emotionally, and mentally will come as the result of a plan and a vision.

AFTER THE VISION

After you get the vision, what do you do with it? Some people rejoice in ideas, but they do not rejoice in the implementation of those ideas. The church is full of such people. They always have good ideas and they are always excited about them. ; They are also excited about the prospect of the next project. The problem is that they never get around to implementing the idea of carrying out the project. I do not want you to be one of those people. You could take my advice and write your vision and life plan in a nice little notebook and carry it with you everywhere. But if you do not "work your plan," it will remain in your notebook for the next five years with no implementation. Put a timetable on your vision. You should know when you are going to implement your plan and how you are going to work it out. So, how do you "work your vision?" How do you make the vision applicable to your life? Let us look to Nehemiah's story one more time for an answer. Nehemiah was a man who did not sit on his vision. He received a vision, and he worked it out. He had a vision, and he worked toward it diligently. Studying Nehemiah gives you a definite course of action for implementing a vision.

1. QUESTIONS PRODUCE VISION

Finding your vision starts when you begin to ask questions. Nehemiah asked a question. He said, "How are the brethren back home?" When he was made aware of their condition, something began to rise in him. He began to be burdened and convicted. Like Nehemiah, you need to begin to ask some questions— questions that would help you understand what is supposed to be done. One of my church members has a hearing problem. Because of the questions, he asked about his own condition, this man developed a vision to create something that will help people who cannot hear well enough to enjoy a movie. He is working diligently on that vision because it was born out of a burden that people who cannot hear should be able to experience the pleasures of life. His questions revolved around finding out how he could make life better for deaf people, and he came up with an idea that is working. This man's questions produced his vision.

48

Begin asking questions. Ask questions about whatever moves you. You might see little children who are impoverished and think something needs to be done about their situation. You may see children who are being neglected or abused by their parents, and you begin to cry. Your emotional response may mean that God is trying to plant a seed of vision within you. Do something about what moves you; make something happen. Ask yourself: How can this be better? You may ask an even better question: what can I do to make things better? Questions help you develop a vision.

Many Christians become super-spiritual when thinking about their vision. They think of Moses and the burning bush. In their minds' sight, they see Moses walking in the wilderness and suddenly coming upon a bush that burns but is not consumed. They mentally hear the booming voice that speaks to Moses from the bush: "Moses, take your shoes off." They think, "Now, that's vision." So, the super-spiritual Christian waits for his burning bush to come, as if that is God's only means of communication with His people. We do not know what we are supposed to do because the booming baritone has not spoken to us yet. Your vision may not come to pass that way. It might come by asking questions. Orville and Wilbur Wright wanted to know how they could travel from point "A" to point "B" faster. They wanted to be like the birds in the sky; but they had to wonder, "Can this really work? Can this thing fly?" Because of the Wright brothers' questions, we can get on a jet today and fly around the world. Questions, many times, produce a vision. Begin by asking some questions about your life. How can I make the quality of my life better? How can I get the result that I desire? How can I be fulfilled before I die? Question what is around you.

2. SERVING OR HELPING OTHERS

A God-given vision always centers on people outside of yourself. Even though you are developing your life plan and your vision, you must realize that God's creatures are made to be interdependent. Because human beings are not "islands," we are naturally dependent on each other. Your life was created to bless somebody else's life. Whatever your vision is, it is going to be tied to blessing somebody else, helping somebody else, or ministering to somebody else. Ask, "What can I do to bless humanity? What can I do to make a difference for humanity? What can I do to help the world be a better place?" Decide that you want to make a difference. That process of questioning and deciding helps you to develop a vision.

Most inventions that really help to make life better for mankind did not come from selfish desires, like riches or fame. Most inventions are geared toward the greater vision of solving problems. Your vision must be attached to a greater vision, a greater good. Your vision may not be what other people call "big." Your vision may be that you want to be a godly parent as you raise your children. It might be that you want to be a schoolteacher who makes a difference in the lives of your students. You may have a vision of being a faithful Sunday school teacher whose efforts touch the life of someone who grows up to do great things. What are you supposed to do with your life? You must find the answer to that question. If God has given you a gift, you must understand how He wants you to use that gift. Your questions will lead you to your vision, and once you identify it, you must wait for the proper timing.

3. WAIT FOR THE PROPER TIMING

Nehemiah amazes me. His vision came in the month of Chisleu, but nothing happened until the month of Nissan. That's a period of four months. During that time, Nehemiah did nothing. He did not move until his time had come. Just like Nehemiah, we have to understand that there is a time for every vision. Sometimes the burden comes and you just cannot move yet. Sometimes you know what you want to do, but you cannot touch it right now. Maybe the resources are not in place, or you just do not have the time. If your time has not come yet, hold on to the vision. While you are waiting, you can still act. You can pray, you can plan, and you can develop your vision. While you are still waiting, you have to believe that God is working; He's in the background making things happen to launch your vision.

4. PRAY, PLAN, PREPARE AND KEEP A GOOD ATTITUDE

I'll never forget when I was called to preach. In 1987, the Lord spoke to me clearly. I did not want to be one of those preachers who just started preaching one day. I said, "God, I've seen a lot of preachers who didn't do right. If you're calling me to preach, I really need to know what you've got in store for me." So, for three weeks, I sought God, and I felt inside that He wanted me to preach. Because I still wanted to be sure, I locked myself up in my office at Alabama State University so that I could hear from God. The Lord spoke to me clearly in an internal, distinct voice. He said, "Son, I've called you, and I've glorified you. Go and do what you've been called to do."

Once I knew that God had called me to preach, that was all I needed. I joined Deeper Life Bible Church, and the first thing I wanted my pastor to know was that I was called to preach. I remember the first time I met him. I was with another man named Chris Ethridge. They were talking, but I had no idea what their conversation was about because I had only one thing on my mind—this pastor needed to know I was a preacher. I wanted him to know my calling because I wanted to preach! Finally, Chris, who was standing next to me, said, "Oh yeah, and he's a preacher too." I realized he was talking about me and thought, "Praise the Lord; that's it. I know I will be preaching next Sunday."

Soon, my pastor called me in to give me my first assignment. He said he did not want me to keep sitting down anymore. Of course, I was thinking, "Praise the Lord. It's about to happen." He said that he needed me to work in the tape ministry. Even though I was disappointed, I said, "Yes, sir. I'll be glad to do that for you." He left me there for nearly two years when he called me for another assignment. He said, "I think it's time for you to leave the tape ministry alone. There are some students at Tuskegee University that we need to pick up for church services. Would you go there in the church van and take them?" I said, "Yes, sir." I drove the church van for another two years. Finally, my pastor began to let me preach every four or five months. I kept thinking that there was some kind of problem with my situation. I knew I had heard from God. Jesus Himself had spoken to me and said, "I've called you, and I've glorified you." But my pastor had me driving the church van more than he allowed me to preach. I thought, "This can't be God!" Today, I can tell you that it truly was God.

During that testing time, I did not understand that even after God has given you a vision, He continues to work behind the scenes preparing for the manifestation of it. Had my pastor released me into ministry when I wanted to be released , I would have been anointed to "found" a church and then "confound" that church. I was not ready. God's wisdom dictated that I wait for His timing. During that waiting period, I still knew that I was going to preach. In my mind, I was preaching; in my heart, I was preaching; and all over *I was preaching;* yet God did not release me into ministry. I then went through a period of frustration. I watched as other pastors in my denomination were sent out to other states and other fields to fulfill their visions. I said, "God, something is wrong. Remember me, O Lord! Don't leave me stuck in Montgomery!" Little did I know how God was preparing a place for me. Everybody else was being sent out, but God had a plan for me to pastor this church, so I was "stuck" in Montgomery. I did not know that one day God would send my pastor to New York to be our Bishop and that my pastor would turn his church over to me. God did not tell me that in advance. God does not always tell you everything about a vision because He wants you to trust Him to bring the vision to pass in His own time and in His own way.

While I was waiting and wondering, God was allowing me to mingle with the people that I was to pastor. He gave us that time to get to know each other; our hearts were joined together. God was preparing the way for His vision, but I could not see it because of my frustrations. The test taught me that every vision has a time. If you have a vision that you cannot do anything about right now, do not abandon it. Do not become frustrated. Instead, pray, plan, prepare, and keep a good attitude.

Nehemiah had his own time of waiting. During that time, the Bible says that he was in the king's presence, and he was "sad." *Sad* is a lot different from *mad*. Nehemiah could have waited in anger. After all, King Artaxerxes was partly responsible for the plight of his people. Nehemiah could have had an "attitude" with the king. Instead, he became sad. He did not become angry.

Studying Nehemiah's actions can help any of us who are waiting for a vision to be manifested. While you wait, you must guard your heart; do not let a root of bitterness spring up in you. If God has not released you to minister yet, do not become so frustrated that you get ahead of God. If God has not moved in your finances, or marriage, or whatever promise He has made to you, you still have to watch your heart. It is all right to want your blessing to come, but it is not all right to become angry with God if He makes you wait. You cannot stop serving God because you are disappointed. Even in times of disappointment, God is still your source. Do not look at the *person* who seems to be keeping you from your blessing.

If you desire a promotion at your job and your boss has not given it to you yet, do not become angry with him. If you are a Christian, it is not your boss that is in control of your life anyway. Do you understand that if God wanted you to be promoted, nobody in hell or earth could stop your promotion? The Bible says promotion does not come from the north, south, east, or west (Psalm 75:6); God is the one who puts one up and another down. So, if what you desire has not happened, talk to God.

The Bible says there is a time and a purpose for every season under heaven. "A time to be born, a time to die, a time to plant, and a time to pluck up that which is planted." (Ecclesiastes 3:1-8) There's summer, there's spring, there's fall, and there's winter. Just as each season in nature must wait its turn, so must you. You cannot rush your season. You cannot speed up destiny. The children of Israel were in slavery for 430 years. God said. "I will release you, but I will release you when the time is right." You may be in a waiting season right now; if so, you must keep the right attitude and be faithful where you are. Nehemiah could have had an attitude. He could have become angry and refused to do his job of serving the king. Instead, he kept his integrity; he continued doing his job while God was doing His.

Part of God's preparation of your vision is to bring others into your life who may have an effect on your attaining the promise. If you are so caught up in your frustrations that you push everyone away with your attitude, you might just find that you have caused those who are supposed to help with your vision to run away from you. Nagging and complaining could be a turn-off to the person that God has in your life to bless and help you fulfill your vision. The very king that Nehemiah would have angered had he been bitter was the very one God used to fulfill Nehemiah's vision. A good attitude could bring you a good favor. Remember God's attitude toward you: "*I know the thoughts that I think towards you, thoughts of peace and not of evil, to give you an expected end*" (Jeremiah 29:11). God knows how to masterfully work out our end. He knows the end of everything we need to be. Many times, God will give us a vision of our "end," but he does not always tell us how He will get us there. He does not always tell us about every storm, trial, mountain, or speed bump that you will face on your journey. Such tests are a part of your character-building process.

No matter what tries to detour you or distract you from your ordered path, stay focused on your vision. While you are waiting for the vision to come to pass, be faithful and trustworthy in doing the work to which you are assigned. It may be that you are in your toilet-cleaning season; decide to be the best toilet cleaner ever. Cleaning those toilets may be a major step in helping to build the character you need to fulfill your vision.

5. BE THE BEST; DO YOUR BEST

I love the story of Les Brown. Before he became a nationally known speaker, he wanted to work at a radio station. He wanted the job so badly that he would go to the station every day and ask the manager if he had any openings. Each day the response was, "I already told you we weren't hiring." Les would respond, "I know, but it's another day; somebody might have died." Despite the rejections, Les held on to his vision. He began to prepare himself. He would sit at home and practice in his mind what he would do when he got that job. He persisted in contacting the manager for a long period of time. One day, he finally realized his vision. The announcer who was supposed to be on the air got drunk and had to be pulled off the air. Les finally got his chance to fill in. Because he had been practicing for years, Les was ready. He got on the radio and just began talking. Brown's small break was the beginning of a career that has brought him international fame.

Learn a lesson from Les Brown. During your waiting season, be the best you can be and do the best you can do. Make friends with everybody. Love everybody. Do not turn your back on anybody. Do not turn people off. Do not say, "I don't need them. I don't need her. Who is she?" You have to understand that, wherever you need to be, other people will help you get there. Develop integrity while you wait. Ecclesiastes 7:1 says, "A good name is better than precious ointment." Part of having a good name is having the integrity to do your best at whatever job you are given. Be faithful and be trustworthy, even in seemingly small things. God says, if you are faithful over a few things, you will rule over many things (Luke 16:10). Waiting is a good position for developing faithfulness.

6. KNOWING WHEN IT'S TIME TO MOVE

One way to know when it is time to act on your vision is that the burden of it begins to consume you. It becomes a "fire shut up in your bones" (Jeremiah 20:9). In Nehemiah 2:1, Nehemiah is in the presence of the king. The Bible says that he had never been sad before in the king's presence. Why was he sad now? He was so burdened by the plight of his people that he could not hold his emotions in. So, his face was sad. In other words, it had gotten to the point where he knew that the time had come that he had to do something about the plight of his people. The knowledge of their circumstances was consuming him. If your vision is beginning to consume you, it may be moving you to action.

A second way you know that it is time to move is when things start falling into place. Notice that the king asked Nehemiah, "What's going on with you?" Nehemiah said, "How can I be happy when my people are messed up back home." Then the king said, "What do you want me to do for you?" So, things started falling into place for Nehemiah. He was able to ask the king for what he needed to fulfill his vision, and the king gave him what he requested. Nehemiah got what he needed because it was time. The same thing will happen to you. When it is time for your vision to be fulfilled, God will put people in place to help you get just what you need to bring your vision to pass.

7. COUNTING THE COST

Luke 14:28 says, " *There's no man who should build something who will not sit down first and count the cost, to see if he has enough to finish it.*" Please use wisdom and assess what your vision will cost you in time and energy. Ask if your family can handle the cost. You cannot develop a life plan without determining how it will affect your wife, your children, and others for whom you are responsible. Your waiting season is a good time to count the cost. After you come up with your plan, you should ask, "Can I really do this? Can I really accomplish this? Can I really make this happen?"

Whatever you do is going to cost you. People always want the anointing. Some of my members even say they want the same anointing I have. They say, "Pastor, lay hands on me and download, transfer by the Holy Ghost, the anointing God has upon your life." But do they really want my anointing? Do they really want to pay the same price I paid to get the anointing that I have? You will pay some kind of price for everything that you get from God. You may look at the life of T.D. Jakes as an example. Some feel that this man rose to international prominence overnight. **That is a lie.** If you ever hear his life story, you will see that he went through many struggles to get where he is today. Every successful person has a story behind their glory. Even Jesus had a price to pay. Not everyone is willing to "take up His cross." Matthew 20:21 tells us of a woman who came to Jesus and asked for favor for her two sons. The **mother** asked that when Jesus got to heaven, he would allow one son to sit on His right hand and the other on His left. Jesus said, "Are you able to drink the cup?" He was asking if they were willing to pay the same price for the glory that Jesus himself was willing to pay. Remember, there is a cup before the crown; there is a story before the glory.

What is your vision? You may say, "I want to be a medical doctor. I have to help people." Praise the Lord. Your desire is honorable, but the road to becoming a doctor is not easy. You will find yourself needing a hefty quantity of caffeine for all of those late study nights, not to mention the sleepless nights of internships. So, there's a story with the glory. Count the cost. Do not just look at the finished structure without also looking at how many bricks it took to build it. Do not just look at where you are going without trying to determine what it is going to take to get you there. There is a cost. Sit down and say, "Can I really do this? Is it in me to do this? Can my family handle it? Can I handle it?" You have to count the cost.

8. DON'T BE DISTRACTED

Another aspect of fulfilling your vision is ignoring distractions. You must be especially careful of distractions that come while you are waiting for your promise. You can be distracted in many ways. Even opportunities can be distractions. You do not want to be doing a good thing and then leave the God thing. It can be very easy to leave a vision that seems to be not going right to follow after a distraction. Such a detour can hinder your fulfillment of the real vision. Instead of following every opportunity, check to see if the opportunity is in line with your vision.

Be focused. Sometimes criticism can be a distraction. Do not think that everybody will support your vision. They may criticize you and say you are not even qualified to do what you want to do. But you cannot be distracted by the criticism of others. Do not let what others say cause you to be afraid. Whatever your vision is, keep pressing in.

Nehemiah was highly criticized. There were two people, Sanballat and Tobiah, who criticized Nehemiah: *"If these people build these walls, a little fox might touch it and the walls will fall down."* They laughed at Nehemiah. They joked about him, but the Bible says Nehemiah kept the people on task. Despite the negative words that were spoken about them, the people kept on building until the walls were finished. I cannot emphasize this point enough.

Your vision may be suffering because of words that were spoken to you or over you, perhaps while you were growing up. They have become a barrier, a hindrance to fulfilling your destiny.

You may be allowing criticism to keep you from doing what God has put in your spirit to do. If so, you need to shake that off. Everybody who did something great was criticized. People like the Wright brothers, Thomas Edison, and Benjamin Franklin were all told that they could not do what they dreamed of doing, but these men learned to press on. Because of their fortitude, we now have modern conveniences such as airplanes, electricity, and even radio and television. It is said that President Kennedy was told there was no way that a man could walk on the moon. Despite the critics, the space program continued, and man did walk on the moon. Negative choices may have had you bound. Do not let them hinder you; keep on pressing on.

Another distraction is a word called " *compromise.* "Don't try to bring your vision to pass through compromise. You do not have to help God out. He is quite capable of making things work on His own. If God promised you a certain job, do not lie on an application to get it. That is not how your vision should happen. If you are in business and God has promised that it will be profitable, do not cheat your customers or cheat on your taxes to realize more "profit." That is not God's way. Suppose God has promised that you are going to make CDs of your music and have a national music ministry. Should you compromise your principles to sign a record deal with a company that wants you to leave out names like "Jesus" and "God" when you sing? That kind of crossover decision could bring you millions of dollars, but it is a compromise. The only thing you ought to crossover is take the *cross* over into the realm of your ministry. Compromise can kill your vision.

Another vision killer is " counterfeit." If you have a vision from God, you must be aware that a counterfeit method of fulfillment will present itself to you. The counterfeit may get the job done, but it will not be God's fulfillment. The counterfeit always precedes the real thing. That is why you must be focused. You must have a clear mental picture of what God has for you. That picture will keep you from being fooled by a counterfeit that does a good job of imitating the real thing. The counterfeit usually has a spirit of compromise with it. It tries to get you to take shortcuts that cause you to set aside your principles. It is impossible to reach a godly destiny through immoral means. The shortcut may be tempting, especially if you have waited a long time for your promise to come.

Even in business, you must follow godly guidelines. You cannot set up a partnership with someone who does not have the same mindset as you do. The Bible says, *"Do not be unequally yoked together with unbelievers"* (2 Corinthians 6:14). That same principle applies to marriage. If God has promised you a mate, He will not send you someone who does not believe in Him or who does not attend church regularly as you do. He wants you to be equally yoked with somebody who is saved. Now, if you are already married and your spouse is not saved, that is different. The Bible has different directions for those circumstances. But if you are single, do not even consider marrying someone who is not of the same faith; that is clear from Scripture.

Whatever God has promised you, do not try to help Him out. He really does not need your help. When it is time for your vision to come to pass, He does it. We don't have to lie, we don't have to cheat, and we don't have to do anything wrong. We don't have to do anything. All we have to do is let God have his way. Resist the temptation to do things that are immoral to help your vision come to pass.

Nehemiah's example should help you as you prepare for your vision and then begin to work out the steps to achieve it. We are going to see how Nehemiah's story can help us in more ways in the next few chapters.

PREPARING FOR YOUR LIFE PLAN

Here are some questions for you to use from the principles learned in Nehemiah's story. Put these principles into your historical timeline in context with receiving your vision plan and what to prepare for while you work toward it.

1. How successful do you think your life has been thus far? Think of it in terms of the different facets of life (business, family, etc., as well as emotional health, spiritual walk, etc.). How much work have you put in to any success you have had to date?

   _____

   _____

   _____

2. Nehemiah asked questions to understand more about his burden for Jerusalem. How can you ask the right questions of the right people to help in your quest?

   _____

   _____

   _____

3. Nehemiah's vision did not center around himself. How can you be sure that even a personal vision for your life centers around others?

   _____

   _____

   _____

4. Nehemiah saw the timing of God throughout the pursuit of his vision. How will you be able to exercise patience when and how God wants to fulfill your vision?

    _____

    _____

    _____

5. Nehemiah kept a good attitude even when the situation was not ideal. Is it easy for you to maintain a good attitude during stress or delay? Why or why not?

    _____

    _____

    _____

6. Nehemiah brought a few people alongside him to catch the vision and move with strength toward it. Is it easy to bring people with you as you move forward toward your goals? How can you be a public relations agent for your vision?

    _____

    _____

    _____

7. Nehemiah gave God his best. Do you find it easy to do your best, or are you tempted to make do when obstacles are in front of you?

    _____

    _____

    _____

8. Nehemiah had to count the cost of fulfilling his vision. How will you assess what your vision may cost you in finances, time, energy, relationships, etc.?

_____

_____

_____

9. Nehemiah faced many distractions to his goal. How easy is it for you to hear criticism? How do you deal with the temptation to compromise? Is it easy for you to discern counterfeit ideas or people?

_____

_____

_____

10. Nehemiah remained focused. How will you be able to cling to God's guidance rather than other good ideas that are not God-given for your vision?

_____

_____

_____

Chapter 5

THE POWER OF IMAGINATION TO YOUR VISION

God has given us a tremendous ability to imagine. Our imagination can be so precise and so well defined that we can actually imagine something and our bodies will react as though it were real. If you don't believe it, just get hungry. I occasionally eat Starburst candy, and whenever I do, my mouth begins to water before I take my first bite. You might have the same reaction to your favorite candy. If I continue to describe your mouth-watering favorite, you might imagine holding it in your hand and opening the wrapper. In your mind, you bring the morsel to your mouth, and just the thought of it makes your saliva glands begin to work overtime. You do not have the actual candy in your mouth, but just the "vision" of it causes your body to react.

Imagination is a tool that gives you the power to experience what is not real as though it were real. That is why God's Word says, "As a man thinketh in his heart, so is he" (Proverbs 23:7). The mind does not always know the difference between reality and fiction when it has a clear mental image. The mind's failure to grasp that difference is the reason pornography is so dangerous. You may say what you are reading or watching is not real; it is words or pictures. In your mind, it is real. That is why while watching a picture, you can experience things in your body that will affect you in a certain way, even though you are not actually engaged in any of the activities you see. Pornography is a big trap, and if you continue to deal with it, you will end up in a spiritual prison (which is bondage). Even though pornography is readily available today, especially on the Internet, you have to avoid that black hole. Pornography is like a drug. You start with a little, but soon that is not enough. You have to have something stronger and stronger. Before long, you find yourself in a prison of your own making—a prison in which you never thought you would be involved. So, do not even open your mind to receiving the pictures. They are mental mind traps that can hinder or kill your ability to fulfill your vision.

The clear mental image you *do* want to receive is the one that shows you your destiny. You cannot just entrust your life to happenstance. You need to see in your mind's sight what you want your life to look like five years from now. When you have that vision firmly etched in your mind, it brings you joy, passion, motivation, enlightenment, and encouragement.

IMAGINING YOUR VISION HAS GREAT BENEFITS

Having a strong picture in your mind benefits you as you work on your vision from conception to completion. Here are some ways you will benefit:

1. It makes you dream big. God's vision will always be bigger than what you feel you can accomplish.
2. It brings continuity. The picture brings stability and connection to the vision.
3. It provides direction and purpose. The vision pushes your motivation forward.
4. It brings increased interest and commitment. You will find the vision brings fulfillment even during the journey.
5. It provides an acceptable change. It helps you want to adapt to the change your vision will bring.
6. It allows you to reject opportunities. It brings boundaries to what you say yes or no to during the process.
7. It brings openness. Your imagination opens your mind to possibilities you never thought of before you saw your vision.
8. It causes encouragement. Even in difficult circumstances, your vision inspires you daily.
9. It inspires confidence. As your vision becomes established, your mental picture becomes a surety that you are on the right path.
10. It promotes loyalty. Your mental picture brings faithfulness to bear toward the vision's fulfillment. To let your vision die is unacceptable.
11. It creates efficiency. Instead of wandering and not heading anywhere, you have a clear path and a set of goals ahead of you. This helps you push distractions out of the picture.
12. It increases productivity. Your efficiency brings your output to a higher level. This helps you see each step as a victory.

NEHEMIAH'S IMAGINATION

Nehemiah's vision kept him going even when the critics showed up. In Nehemiah's imagination, he could actually see the walls going up. Despite the seemingly overwhelming task that lay before him and his people, Nehemiah was able to stay focused and encouraged because he *saw* where he was going. Those walls were vital to the protection and continued viability of his home nation, so Nehemiah could not afford to lose his hope. His vision extended past the building of the walls; he also saw the nation's government being restored. Because he had a vision, a mental picture of what should be, Nehemiah set out to accomplish it.

But that isn't all Nehemiah's imagination did for his vision. Throughout the process of pursuing each goal within the framework of that vision, Nehemiah's picture of a finished wall helped keep him on task. And this was in spite of the distance, lack of resources, and fewer personnel that would have been ideal. Then there were the naysayers, those who wanted to completely thwart Nehemiah's goals. These people were not just trying to influence Nehemiah, but the workers he did have. He had to spread his imagination to his company of builders, stirring their imaginations to picture the completion of their toil.

YOUR IMAGINATION IN THE PROCESS

Just as Nehemiah used the picture of his vision to his advantage, you can use your imagination at every stage of your vision's journey. First, use it to capture the vision God has given to you. Let it help you stand upon your watch. Second, use your mental picture to document your vision. Third, your vision can help you simplify the vision for others. Although you may need to see all the components, others who will walk with you need a highly focused version. This is how you "make your vision plain." Use your imagination to communicate your vision to others. This may include those whose resources you need. It may also include those who will help you carry out the vision. A picture is "worth 1000 words." This helps others who "may run that read it." So that others do not begin to distort your vision with their ideas, be sure to keep a picture of what you see before them.

Next, your imagination is needed to discern the proper timing. When you have a mental picture, you can recognize when situations, resources, and support are in alignment with that picture. Then, you use your vision to produce a plan. This plan must adhere to your overall mental picture of what should be done. The plan needs imagination as you see the journey as important for the growth of everyone involved as much as the end result.

As you proceed through the steps and goals, you may find your vision needs some revision. You will be able to recognize how your mental picture changes as your imagination sees the changes. Remember, we only see in part, and this truth means we may have to hone in on the best vision possible during the process.

PREPARING FOR YOUR LIFE PLAN

Here are some questions for you to use the principles learned from Nehemiah to put your historical timeline in context with receiving your vision plan and what to prepare for while you work toward it.

11. How have you used your imagination in seeing pictures of the visions God has given to you?

_____

_____

12. As we are made in God's image, we see that God's image is everywhere in the variety that is offered in our world in plants, animals, terrain, and seasons. How is your imagination a part of you displaying the glory of God?

_____

_____

13. As you look at your historical timeline, can you see when God gave you a clear mental picture in order to strengthen His vision in your life?

_____

_____

14. As you prepare your life's plan going forward, how can you stimulate your imagination God-ward during the journey?

_____

_____

Chapter 6

OPPOSITION WILL COME

As you form your vision, you may expect that, since it is God-given, you will see circumstances and resources begin to quickly come into alignment. But early in the establishment of your vision, there are unseen elements at work in your heart to kill your vision. If your vision is from God, then it is to be expected that Satan will want to thwart that which is in your heart. But to Satan's demise, God says that He will make all things (including mistakes, character issues, and unforeseen trouble) work for your good. (Romans 8:28)

Looking at any vision killers will help you on multiple fronts. You will build your character closer to that of Jesus, you will undo the plans of Satan, and you will have a testimony as to how this vision has changed you. Here are six vision killers:

1. Tradition:Tradition is a reflection of the past. A vision is always a reflection of the future.

2. Fear: Past failures often press you to fear reaching for the stars again.

3. Stereotypes: (someone with your background, skin color, gender can't...)

4. Complacency: Rev 3:15-18 – Lukewarm makes the vision spoil like sour milk.

5. Fatigue:Vision calls for a tremendous amount of faith and energy. Seeking a vision when you are exhausted will create challenges.

6. Short-term thinking: We deplete the past to enjoy the present at the expense of the future.

Right after you set out to work on your vision, you can expect some other kinds of opposition. Whatever vision you have for your life, whatever you determine to do, it is not going to be smooth sailing. The world itself is full of opposites. There is the day, but there is also the night. We have times of laughter, but we must also experience pain. We have our seasons of joy, but we also have seasons of sorrow. Some things are easy, but others are difficult. This rule of opposites or oppositions also pertains to vision. You will run into some kind of difficulty, especially if you are trying to do something for God. Realizing the potential for difficulty will help you to be better prepared for the process of fulfilling your vision.

DEFENDING THE VISION

You have seen how Nehemiah is an example of a visionary. So far, you have read how he conceived the vision and how that conception propelled him into action. You read how he found favor with the king and received the materials and people he needed to rebuild the walls around his homeland. You examined how he presented his plan to the people who caught his vision and began to work. Rejoin him as the wall goes up and their enemies are trying to tear it down. Learn from Nehemiah how you might deal with opposition to your own visions.

Nehemiah 4:1 starts with the word "but." Have you ever started to do something positive and a " but" came along? Everything is fine, " but." I love this job, "But." That "but" gets in the way. Like many of us, when Nehemiah began his vision, everything seemed to be going well. He had the king's favor, the people responded to his plans with zeal, and he had the materials he needed to get the job done. Nehemiah was watching his vision become a reality until a big "but" came along: "*But it came to pass, that when Sanballat heard that we builded the wall, he was wroth, and took great indignation, and mocked the Jews*" (Nehemiah 4:1).

Nehemiah and his people were facing strong opposition. They were the targets of Sanballat's mocking and criticism. When God gives you a vision or a job to do, He does not always warn you of the opposition ahead. He shows you the blueprint of what is to be, but He does not always show you the process. God shows you the finished product, but He often does not show you the months and even years of the *process* you have to go through to complete your "product."

One of the first things that you are going to have to deal with when you set out to accomplish your vision is people who do not see what you see. In Nehemiah's case, Sanballat and Tobiah were governors who lived nearby, and they were accustomed to being the heads of that whole region. They felt threatened by

Nehemiah's leadership of the people, so they mocked the people's efforts. They hated the progress that the Jews were making in rebuilding the walls.

As you work on your vision, you will find that not everyone wants to see you succeed. Not everyone will want to see you prosper in what you do. Not everybody wants you to get that raise. Not everybody wants your family to be happy. Not everybody wants to see you married. That is why you cannot share your vision with everyone. Some people will give you the "if I were you" advice. Yet they know that if they were in the same situation, they would not follow the advice they are giving. You must choose your confidantes carefully. You cannot be like Joseph in the Bible. He had a dream about his future and just could not wait to share it with his brothers. He told them, "Last night I had a dream and all of you were bowing down to me." That was not what his older brothers wanted to hear. So, they not only mocked him, but they also sold him into slavery. You cannot share your dreams with everyone. I understand that at some point, everybody needs someone to talk to, but you must pray and ask God to show you the person that you can trust. You must limit the sharing of your vision when it is in its initial stages. Criticism at that point could really hinder you from taking the necessary first steps to bring the vision to pass.

FACING YOUR CRITICS

When a vision is first conceived, it may be easy for others to talk you out of pursuing it because all you have is a "what," not a "how." You may tell others that you see yourself as a millionaire, as a pastor of a huge church, or as a best-selling author. All you can tell others is "what" you see, not "how" you plan to get there. People may criticize your desire because they cannot see what you see.

Most new converts have to face this kind of opposition. They become saved and eagerly share their vision of their new lives with those who know them. The newly saved person expects his friends to celebrate the change in their lives . Instead, in many cases, the friends turn into critics. They say, "You'll be back in a few weeks. This won't last." If the new convert sticks to his decision and chooses to spend time in prayer and reading the Word, he may be accused of being a member of a cult. Such criticism comes because the people in his life are still stuck in his past while he is trying to pursue his vision of going to heaven. Many new converts become confused at this point because they cannot understand why their family and friends are not celebrating the positive changes in their lives. The problem is that if your loved ones are not on the same path as you , they cannot "see" your goal.

Nehemiah faced the same problem. The work he was doing was good, but he was criticized. They criticized Nehemiah's character. They criticized his ability. They criticized his commitment. They criticized his sanity. They criticized his competency. You too are going to face criticism. You will encounter people who do not understand you or your vision. People who do not like what you are doing and criticize you for trying, may even attack you. Many others may have one of the six vision killers mentioned above plaguing their own visions and will, by association, begin to implant their specific vision killer on you.

DEVELOPING "STICKY"-ABILITY

When Nehemiah went back to his people, the Bible says he took time to check on everything. He planned, he rode on his horse, and he looked at the rubble. He sized everything up for three days. When he finished, he gave instructions to his people. Everybody was excited. They said, "We'll do whatever you say." Like so many of us, they began their first days of rebuilding by working with all their hearts. Can you imagine them saying, "We're going to rebuild this wall. We're going to make a name for ourselves again. We're going to build on our heritage again . Praise the Lord!"

What they did not know was that the opposition was just around the corner. The opposition had to come because the enemy and life itself do not just step back and let things happen. That is why those who make things happen are those who know how to press through opposition to achieve their goals. The greatest ability is "stick ability"—the ability to stick with something and not give up.

We have to learn that when things get tough, we must get tough, too. We have to be like postage stamps: they stick with a letter until it gets there, and they always stick better when they take a licking. So, even if you are taking a licking, that should make you stick better and get to your destination. Expect opposition. Be prepared for it. It is going to come against your marriage, your business, your vision, your opportunity, your health—whatever the point of attack, the opposition will come to try to take you out. But if you have tenacity, grace, and an understanding that adversity will come, you can press on to your goal. You have to defend your vision.

When people discourage you, they take the courage and ability out of you to accomplish what needs to be accomplished. You are going to have to deal with people's mouths. While some negative words do come from well-meaning people, others have their origin in people who intend to discourage you. People who are jealous of you will talk you down from any positive goal that you might have. Not all of your co-workers want to see you promoted. Not everyone wants to see you blessed. Sometimes people want the blessings for themselves alone. They tolerate you only when you are equal to or "below" them. If you begin to rise above them in your job, your marriage, or your ministry, you may see their jealousy come to the surface. They may begin to criticize you. If you are weak in your vision, then their words can hinder you. Their criticism can hurt you, stop you, and turn you around.

The famous inventor, Thomas Edison, had to face criticism. Some could not believe that it was possible to invent something like the light bulb, but Edison had to ignore those who spoke against his dreams. To reach your goal, you need one deaf ear and one blind eye. You only need to receive half of what you hear and half of what you see. You must learn to sift through what you hear to see what is worth having your attention. You cannot take to heart everything that is said to you. You must weigh even the advice you get from relatives and those in authority over you.

In Nehemiah 4:2, here is what Sanballat and Tobiah said: **"What do these feeble Jews**. Will they fortify themselves? Will they sacrifice?" The question was really, "Who do they think they are? Surely, they can't accomplish this work without bribing God with some kind of sacrifice." This mockery questioned the ability of the people to rebuild the walls. They had a great deal of negativity to overcome. While you may not hear those same questions outright, they may be implied. You may have just finished sharing your heart about what God has put on your heart to accomplish and someone says, "It's going to take a miracle to do that." If you are not careful (and prayerful), those words could keep you from pursuing your vision. Many people are still carrying around the negative words of others, and those words are still having a hindering effect.

Negative words could come from various sources. Those words may have their origins in your childhood. They may be words your parents or some other authority figure said. They may have been words that were spoken to you as a child by other children. Some of us need deliverance from the hurtful words of our past. We need to overcome those things that limit us. We cannot continue to let those things hold us back.

THE FORCE OF FOCUS

How did Nehemiah deal with the words that were spoken against his vision? How did he respond to the mocking comments that even a "fox" could run up on the walls and knock them down? Nehemiah's response was prayer. He said, "God, hear what they are saying about your vision. You turn their reproach upon their own heads." Nehemiah knew that vengeance had to be in God's hands (Romans 12:19). When you have a vision, you do not fight tit for tat with your enemies. You stay focused, and you keep on building. So many times, we want to take vengeance into our own hands.

I have been tested in that area myself. I have had to deal with the anger that comes when someone tells lies about me or when they lie to me. I admit that it was tempting to deal with the situations myself, but I have learned that you can never win by doing that. Even if I had won an argument, I might have lost a soul. I would never have had respect in his eyes again. I could never bear witness to him. I have learned to smile past my emotions and be extra nice to my "enemies." Now, I am no Superman. When I am attacked, I have to counsel myself. I have to remind myself that God is my defense, and I trust that He will deal with the consciences of those who come against me. So, whatever you are going through, just remember that vengeance belongs to God.

When somebody comes up against you, do not argue with the person. When somebody tells you twenty reasons why your vision will not work, do not "curse them out." Just pray and give the situation to God, and He will take care of it. In the meantime, do not stop what you are doing: do not stop building; do not stop writing the book; do not stop writing the poetry; do not stop sowing the seed; do not put down or modify the vision; do not try to build half the wall just because somebody is talking. Do not change a thing; you keep praying and pressing on. You work and let them keep talking. You cannot tame the tongues of others any more than you can tame your own.

I want you to think of the visions that you have been talked out of. What did you not do because someone talked you out of it? I'm not talking about godly counsel, but I am speaking of the negativity that you received from someone else. Is there a dream that you need to resurrect? I don't care if you are eighty-one years old. If it was God's will for you to do it, you may need to go back and pick up the dream that you had put down. When you do, you may need to prepare yourself to face opposition and criticism again.

PREPARING FOR YOUR PLAN

Use the principles learned from Nehemiah to address any opposition that can come against your vision, before you form it, during the process, and as you are ready to complete it. Consider each of these oppositions that came within your historical timeline. Then prepare to address the opposition to your future vision. How has the specific opposition kept you from fulfilling vision in your life thus far? What are some ways you can prepare yourself to get beyond these past responses and be prepared to press beyond them?

1. Tradition

_____

_____

_____

_____

2. Fear

_____

_____

_____

_____

3. Stereotypes

_____

_____

_____

_____

4. Complacency

_____

_____

_____

_____

5. Fatigue

_____

_____

_____

_____

6. Short term thinking

_____

_____

_____

_____

PART 3
BEING PREPARED FOR THE VISION JOURNEY

Chapter 7

DEALING WITH INCREASED WARFARE

"But it came to pass that when Sanballat, and Tobiah, and the Arabians, and the Ammonites, and the Ashdodites, heard that the walls of Jerusalem were made up, and that the breaches began to be stopped, then they were very wroth"
(Nehemiah 4:7).

In this verse, we see Nehemiah facing another " but." At first, his enemies were "wroth" because of his work, but now they have become "very wroth" because of the progress he was making. Sometimes, the more progress you make, the greater the trouble that comes your way. Every round goes higher and higher, and every devil gets bigger and bigger (new levels, new devils). Sometimes, the closer you get to your goal, the opposition against you increases. Things may become more difficult just before your breakthrough comes.

Nehemiah had almost reached his goal when the warfare against him intensified. His enemies rose up on every side. The

Arabs came from the South, the Ammonites from the East, and the Ashdodites came from the West. Nehemiah's enemies literally surrounded him. Have you ever felt that way while working on something God has given you to do? You may have a simple vision of having a peaceful family, gaining prosperity, or just serving God and winning souls. While you work on your goal, you may find yourself surrounded by critics who try to hinder your progress. You must understand how your real enemy, Satan, works. The Bible says that there are three things that the devil comes to do: to steal, to kill, and to destroy. (John 10:10)

1. He will try to steal the vision from your heart before you have the chance to do anything with it.
2. He will try to kill the vision as it is being born.
3. He will try to destroy the vision after it is developed.

Satan's three-pronged attack places you in spiritual warfare. As the warfare intensifies, you may feel surrounded. You may face opposition from a bank, a co-worker, or a fellow church member. You may even face opposition in your home. What do you do when you're surrounded by trouble? You know your first step is to pray, but you cannot pray just any prayer. You must engage in spiritual warfare. Look at Nehemiah 9 again: *"Nevertheless, we made our prayer unto God, and set a watch against them day and night, because of them."*

I have had to counsel people who found themselves surrounded as Nehemiah was. Not too long ago, a pastor and his wife came to me for counseling. These were people who were seasoned in ministry and marriage. They related how they were facing opposition in their church, at home, and in marriage. The pastor said he was so overwhelmed that he was beginning to feel dead to everything, including his marriage. As I listened to them, I asked God to show me what the problem really was. When they finished, I was able to tell them what God had spoken to my heart. I said, "God told me to tell you that you have been so busy that you've neglected to wage spiritual warfare. He says that you've neglected to pray together, and because of that, the enemy has come to steal, kill, and destroy."

My advice was that they enter into thirty days of spiritual warfare. I told them to pray together every day for at least twenty minutes. They were not to argue about or even discuss the situations facing them; they were just to pray together. I told them they had to go beyond the normal "bless me" prayers to actual spiritual warfare. I told them to deal with the devil and send their enemies back where they came from. I told them to call me at the end of thirty days. I think it was about twenty-one days later that I received a call from the pastor and his wife. They said, "Pastor, you're a man of God." They said everything had turned around. The enemy had been defeated in just twenty-one days of seeking God and waging spiritual warfare.

When you find your vision surrounded on all sides, you have to pray a different kind of prayer. You pray in aggressive warfare. It is wrong to assume that because you are facing mountains of opposition that you are not following God's will. Nehemiah was doing the will of God, but his enemies came from everywhere. Nehemiah did not doubt his vision. He went into spiritual warfare.

THE BENEFIT OF TRIALS

Do not think that your troubles, trials, and temptations catch God off guard. God allows them because we grow stronger through them. He does not send the trials, but he does allow them. Our response should be to determine whether we grow through our tests or whether we die from them. For Nehemiah and his people, the fight was an actual physical battle. All the Ammonites, the Asdodites, and the other "ites," were actually coming against them to wage war. Because your battles are usually fought in the spirit, you must learn how to wage spiritual warfare. The Bible says, "*We wrestle not against flesh and blood.*" That means our enemy is not flesh and blood, but rather the "principalities, powers and rulers of the darkness." (Ephesians 6:12)

Your spiritual battle may come through a person, but the real enemy is not usually the person himself. The enemy is the spirit that operates through that person. The devil uses people to get his work done. I will never forget when I learned this in real life experience. I was having one of *those days.* I was a new Christian, and I was going through an extremely intense time of spiritual warfare. I woke up one morning, and it was as if the devil had found my address. Everything went wrong. I went to work that day, and I remember saying to myself, "I don't think I can take another thing." I was under a great deal of pressure.

When I got to work, my boss called me to her office and just let me have it. Only two days before, she had praised me, saying I was one of their greatest employees. Now, she was accusing me of not doing my work; she said I was just walking around praying all the time. I could not believe this was the same woman who had just recently given me such accolades for doing my job so well. Then, it hit me. I realized this new, unwarranted attack was from the devil. So, I just smiled and said, "I'm sorry, Ma'am. What do you want me to do?" After she left, I fully realized that the enemy had come to destroy something God had given to me. I could have responded to her in the same spirit that she spoke to me. I could have let her have it, lost my job, and walked out of that place proud, broke, and stupid. Warfare came, but it was not my boss that I was fighting; it was the enemy. I knew because the very next day she did not remember the incident. I referred to her previous critical remarks and asked if I could do anything to improve. She said, "No. You're fine." She praised me for my performance again. She had been used as a vessel by the enemy. Even though Satan's intent was to destroy me, God allowed that incident to happen to strengthen and teach me. You may expect something similar to happen to you. The enemy will use people against you. Many times, he will use those who are closest to you. Your spouse might be the one he uses. Your children might be the ones. Whatever the form of the hindrance or distraction, remember not to try to "wrestle against flesh and blood." (Ephesians 6:12)

Some of you are dealing with warfare right now. For some, your first reaction may be to try to find a way to escape rather than face the situation. Please take this as a word from the Lord: Warfare is not going to go away unless you deal with it. You do not *ignore* the enemy and expect him to flee; you deal with him. You submit yourself to God, and you resist the enemy. If you go on the offensive and wage your own warfare in the spirit, you will overcome the problems that you face in achieving your goals. You must not back away from the opposition. You must not forsake your vision. When everything comes against you, fight back and defeat your enemy.

WATCHING, PRAYING, AND BUILDING

When spiritual warfare comes, one of the things the devil wants you to do is be so busy fighting him that you no longer build. In Nehemiah 4:8, the enemies decided to come against Jerusalem so the people would come down from the walls to fight. But Nehemiah kept the people focused on the vision. In verse 9, Nehemiah says , "*Nevertheless, we made our prayer unto God, and set a watch against them day and night.*" At first, Nehemiah and the people just prayed; then they set a watch. When your own warfare is going on, you have to do more than pray; you have to set a "watch" against your enemy. The watch is set because the enemy can be so deceptive and so subtle that he might sneak up on you. That is the time when you have to pray more, fast more, and watch your flesh more. Watch where you go, watch your friends, watch your back, watch your front. The enemy wants to destroy your vision, and he will try to do it through any means that he can. You have to watch, pray, fight, and *build.*

DISCOURAGEMENT, LOSS OF STRENGTH AND FATIGUE

"And Judah said, The strength of the bearers of burdens is decayed, and there is much rubbish so that we are not able to build the wall." (Nehemiah. 4:10)

The people of Judah had faced opposition to their efforts to rebuild the wall. They overcame criticism and warfare, but then they became tired. The Bible says, "the strength of the bearers of burdens" (the people who carried the supplies to them) had decayed. Have you ever felt burned out? Have you ever felt that there was a whole lot of work to be done , but you had nothing left inside you to complete the work? In the middle of a vision, just when the plan demands the most effort, your "strength decays." When that happens, you may find yourself becoming discouraged or disheartened. Even the best of us can find ourselves in this position.

The prophet Elijah was a victim of burnout. After he had finished killing the prophets of Baal, Queen Jezebel sent him a threatening message, saying she was going to kill him. Elijah's reaction was to run into the wilderness. He sat under a juniper tree "and requested for himself that he might die" (I Kings 19:4). The verse goes on to say that Elijah had had "enough." Spiritual work is taxing. Physical work is also taxing. There is a limit to what the human body and emotions can take. When you find yourself becoming discouraged and burned out from working on your vision, you must allow God to pull you aside for some recreation, replenishing, and rebuilding of the spirit. If you experience burnout, do not abandon your vision. You may need to refocus. Remember, it is sometimes normal to face discouragement. However, you cannot stay in that condition.

Some of you may be tired now. You may have started on the road to fulfilling your vision, but the road is longer than you had expected, or it may have more of an uphill incline than you were prepared to climb. You may become tired; your spirit may become "decayed." You may get tired of your marriage, your financial situation, or dealing with your children. You may have tried to get closer to God and started climbing the mountain of anointing and grace. You may have heard from God and done all that you knew to do, but you have not been able to make it.

Now you are tired. So, what do you do when you lose strength in the middle of your vision? What do you do when, at the point that strength is required the most, you have none left? First, you have to look outside yourself to the source of unlimited strength, unlimited power, and unlimited potential. Second, regroup and return to the work. In Nehemiah 4:14-15, Nehemiah saw the workers' discouragement, but he would not let the people give up. He told them to "Remember the Lord...and fight" for the vision. Once the people turned back to the right source, they were able to return to work. You must do the same thing during your times of discouragement. Remember that God is the source of your strength. Remember those times that He brought you out before. You may remember what He did for someone else, knowing that He would do the same thing for you. You also have to remember that even though you don't feel Him, you don't sense Him, and you don't see how He can move on your behalf,

He will move and He will deliver you. Our impossibilities are nothing to God. He has been dealing with impossible situations for thousands of years.

When you get to a place that seems to be difficult, remember that God has promised to make your crooked places straight and to make a way through your wilderness (Isaiah 45:2; 42:19). If all you have now is a memory of what God has done for you in the past, then hang on to that memory. Even the memory of a "small" answered prayer can help give you the strength to go on to the next phase of your vision. So, you may be tired. You may be going through something. You may be discouraged, but remember that Jesus Christ is "the same yesterday, today, and forever." (Hebrews 13:8) That means that if He delivered you before, He will do it again. What He did yesterday, He can do today and tomorrow. It is an insult to God to think that He would forsake His children when they need Him most. The Bible says that He began a good work in us, and He will complete that work. That knowledge of God will keep you going when your emotions are drained and your strength is depleted.

Anyone who is a true visionary needs to have a firm knowledge of who God is. In Nehemiah 4:14, God is described as "great and *terrible*." The word "terrible" means awesome. It is the terrible God who renews your strength to continue fighting. When you become weary in doing something that God has given you to do, it may be that you have taken on too much of the vision for yourself. The battle is not yours. It is God's responsibility(2 Chronicles 10:15). While He calls you to do the work, He does not call you to fight your own battles. For the people of Judah, God fought for them and revealed the plans of their enemies.

"And it came to pass, when our enemies heard that it was known unto us, that God had brought their counsel to nought, that we returned all of us to the wall, every one unto his work." Whenever you do something for God, the enemy will "counsel" against you, but you need to know that God will bring your enemies' plans to nothing. God's intervention on your behalf gives you the strength to continue pursuing your vision. When you have a vision that is God-inspired, you must trust Him to tear down every obstacle, and you must keep pressing toward your goal.

STRENGTH IN UNITY

> *"And I said unto the nobles, and to the rulers, and to the rest of the people, The work is great and large and we are separated upon the wall, one far from another" (Nehemiah. 4:19).*

In the middle of the attack against them, Nehemiah saw that the people were scattered all over the wall. He said, "We are divided; we are too far apart." Nehemiah called his people together and gave them a new plan for completing the work. His plan was one of unity. Nehemiah knew that as the people came together, they had a greater chance of keeping their enemies at bay. If your vision involves others, you must be careful that you do not become divided. You need to be "one vision" minded. (Philippians 2:1) Do not allow the enemy to put space between you and those who share in the work of your vision. One of the enemy's major tactics is "divide and conquer." You must be on guard for any signs of division in the ranks and ask God for a plan to restore and maintain unity.

COMPROMISE AND DISTRACTION

"Now, it came to pass... that Sanballat and Geshem sent unto me, saying, Come, let us meet together in some one of the villages in the plain of Ono..." (Neh. 6:1,2).

Another tactic the enemy uses is to cause you to compromise your plan or to be distracted from your work. Nehemiah was nearly finished with the walls when his enemies tried to distract him with a seemingly innocent request for a meeting, but Nehemiah was able to discern their motives. "But they sought to do me mischief." Nehemiah knew that his enemies just wanted to distract him from his work. His response was, "*I am doing a great work, so that I cannot come down; why should the work cease, whilst I leave it, and come down to you?*" (Nehemiah 6:3).

When the enemy finds that he cannot stop you through warfare, cannot hinder you through criticism, and cannot slow you down through discouragement, then he will try to distract you. Usually, that distraction is something that appears to be good, something that appeals to you. There are so many good things that you can do; but if you are not careful, you will be doing so many good things that you will leave out the God things. God may call you to stay home and be a good mother. You know that is the *God* thing He wants you to do, but you see so many *good* things that you could be doing. You begin to volunteer for so many worthy causes that you find yourself distracted from the one thing that God has called you to do. When you are distracted from your vision, the enemy is happy. He knows you are busy, but you are not busy doing the right things.

As a pastor, I face that challenge all the time. All of my work as a pastor is "good," but I constantly ask God, "What do you want me to do right now?" There are always many things I could be doing, but are all of those things part of the vision? I have to be careful how I invest my time. You must also be careful. You must know what your vision is and make sure that you do not allow yourself to be distracted from it.

PREPARING FOR YOUR LIFE PLAN

This chapter has given examples of spiritual warfare that Nehemiah faced and that you may face during the development of your vision and its journey to fulfillment. Develop your own Spiritual Warfare Prayer Guide for your vision. It can be your "go-to" reference tool so that when the warfare comes, you can engage quickly and effectively. Use the Scripture as a prayer or decree against the specific issue you face.

MY SPIRITUAL WARFARE PRAYER GUIDE

Attack	Scripture	Prayer
Steal	1 Samuel 30:8	As God told David to pursue the enemy that stole from Israel, I will not pull back but go on the offensive to recover all that has been lost...
Kill	Psalm 23:4	My vision may go through the valley of the shadow of death, but I will not fear evil, for God is with me...
Destroy	Colossians 2:13-15	Jesus publicly humiliated Satan on the cross. I believe this will undoubtedly expose the enemy to me now...

Surrounded	Ephesians 6:12	Although I may feel surrounded, I know my struggle is not against flesh and blood but against forces of evil...
Retreat	Mark 3:14-15	I have been sent to drive out wicked spirits and advance God's kingdom...
Give Up	Psalm 2:4	Jesus, the Mighty Warrior, has already become the victor of this battle. Jesus laughs at every plan the enemy has plotted against me...
Weariness	2 Corinthians 12:8	When I am weary, I know that God's strength is made perfect through my weakness...
Division	Philippians 2:1	I will stay close to those who believe in the vision and encourage us to be of one mind and heart...
Way is Crooked	Isaiah 45:7	Even though the vision seems to take detours, God will make each crooked place become straight...

In a Desert	Isaiah 42:19	When I feel like things are dry and not moving or growing toward the completion of the vision, I remember that God will make a way through my wilderness...
Battle Too Hard	2 Chronicles 20:15	When the battle weighs heavily upon me, I remember that the battle is ultimately the Lord's. The vision is from Him, and He will bring it to pass...
Distraction	Proverbs 4:25	When distractions pull and tug at me, I will fix my gaze directly before the Lord...
Criticism	2 Corinthians 10:3-5	When the naysayers criticize me, I will not fight with words as they do. I will not war after the flesh, but in righteousness, pursue my course...

SPIRITUAL WARFARE DECREES

My God is greater than any problem I may have. He is always greater, and I choose to worship Him while the battle rages around me. I will overcome the enemy just as Jesus did. (1 John 4:4)

Evil is overcome by good. I focus on the goodness of God in all things and respond to situations with the goodness of the Lord. (Romans 12:21)

The weapons of my warfare are not the same as the world's weapons. I choose a different way to fight. I fight with divine power that demolishes strongholds, arguments, and pretensions that set themselves up against the knowledge of God. I take captive every thought I had to make them obedient to Christ. (2 Corinthians 10:3-5)

I will not shrink back but stand my ground, using truth, righteousness, and peace to advance against the enemy. The sword of the spirit, the Word of God, will come to bear in every situation. (Ephesians 6:14-17)

I will not allow warfare against the enemy to deter me from my vision. In the all-powerful name of Jesus, I send the enemy back to where he came from. He shall not return but be bound to his domain. I have the blood and the name of Jesus Christ, son of the Most High God, surrounding me. (James 4:7)

I know who is greater than any power the enemy manifests – my God is greater. He has given His power to me, so I can command the enemy to leave without any manifestation. I have the authority in Christ to respond to the enemy. (Luke 10:19)

Chapter 8

THE FUTURE AWAITS YOU

What are you going to do? No, I mean it! What are you going to do with all of the resources God has given you? Your time, talent, effort, energy, and vision. It changes everything when we really realize that our future is up to us. Human nature loves to pass the blame. We got it from our parents, Adam and Eve. When God confronted Adam after he ate the fruit, Adam replied (my paraphrase): " This woman you gave me, gave me the fruit and I ate it." Since then, that gene has been passed on to all humanity. It's always someone else's fault. The truth is that no one is to blame for our lack of success but us. The remaining years of your life are in your hands. What are you going to do with it? Let me give you a few suggestions.

FORGETTING AND PRESSING

I In writing a letter to the Philippian church, Paul the Apostle shared one of the secrets of his success.

Philip. 3:13-15
Brethren, I count not myself to have apprehended: but this one thing I do, forgetting those things which are behind, and reaching forth unto those things which are before, I press toward the mark for the prize of the high calling of God in Christ Jesus. Let us therefore, as many as be perfect, be thus minded: and if in anything ye be otherwise minded, God shall reveal even this unto you.

What counsel! What an advise! What Paul did is what we must do. We must forget the things that are behind us and press forward to the things that are before us. Forget about yesterday and concentrate on tomorrow. Forgetting about yesterday doesn't mean we forget the lessons that history teaches us, for that would doom us to repeat them. It does mean not allowing the mistakes of yesterday to slow us down today. It doesn't matter what your résumé currently says. What matters most is what it will say. Start writing your résumé now. Chart out the next days, months, and years of your life and follow it intensely. Begin to reach for the things that are in front of you. Press toward *"the mark."* What is that mark? Only you will know. But I do know that your vision is the ticket to it. Press toward the mark for the prize of your high calling in Christ.

Let me put it another way, "go for it." Or as Nike puts it, "just do it." No more excuses. Excuses are stepping-stones to failure. Just "Be." Don't just dream. Become that business owner or that talented teacher. Be that anointed writer or that Holy Spirit-inspired poet. Come on! Write the song and publish the CD. Start the church or build the house. Write the article. You say, "but what if no one publishes it?" I say, what if someone does publish it? Sir, go ahead and get married and start your family. The fact that your last girlfriend was unfaithful should not cripple the rest of your life. Young lady, go ahead! Counsel those troubled teens; your mistakes as a teenager have given you the experience to help others.

No knight is coming on a white horse, and Publisher's Clearing House is not coming to your house with a million dollars. You rise up and take your future into your own hands and stop waiting for "it." So many people live and die waiting for "it." I say to you, don't wait for "it," but make "it." Make "it" happen. Go and find "it" because "it" probably won't find you.

YOUR CURRENT RESOURCES

God tells us that we need to "know ourselves." (Proverbs 13:16) Through our historical timelines, we can immediately see some of these resources.

1. Skills taught through parents or education;
2. Talents developed during childhood through adults;
3. Spiritual training from the church, family, or others;
4. Events that proved your capabilities.

There are also resources that are not as visible but still a part of your history. Some of these will have both positive and negative areas . The positive ones are ready for use. The negative ones are the ones where you are still working to make them assets.

1. Emotional fortitude
2. Mental aptitude

3. Physical capability
4. Stamina for the long-haul
5. Spiritual gifts
6. Fruit of the spirit that others have seen in you

No one has the exact same history that you do, nor the exact set of resources. The uniqueness of who you are is exciting! God is ready to help you unfold your future legacy.

JUST DO IT

Your life plan is important. It is your written vision. Start writing it today. No angel is going to come down from heaven to write this script for you. You have to develop it, and you have to be determined to follow it. Can you imagine what a document like this could do for your life? If you lose focus, the plan will help you get back on track. Your plan gives your life direction, focus, and motivation. It brings productivity and purpose to your life. Now, write your vision and make it plain, so you may run when you read it. The next section has tools to help you create your own plan. The first is a list of areas and how to develop them. The second is a blank vision planner for you to use as your response to the first tool. The last tool is a sample of what my personal vision may look like to help you with yours.

FINISH THIS BOOK

You know, I think I will leave this chapter just like your life is right now, unfinished. I can't complete this chapter because you are the completion of it. You are the one who has to write the remaining paragraphs. Will it be a joy for me to read them, or will it be a drudge? I want to read the end of chapter eight. Contact me. I don't care if it's a year from now or ten years from now. If the Lord grants us life, please contact me. Let me read the completion of this chapter. I want to hear about what you do with this information. Email me at ksearcy1@gmail.com Blessings! And best wishes on your journey to success.

APPENDICES

APPENDIX A

DEVELOPING A LIFE PLAN

W hen you begin to develop your life plan, you must keep two things in mind: your goal and your timeline. Your plan must build toward some kind of destination. That destination is tied to your vision. Your plan also needs to be driven by a timeline to keep you on task. So, having a goal and a timeline are vital elements in any life plan. Highlight areas you should put in your plan and take notes in the margins. Then utilize these in APPENDIX B.

THE GOAL: The first area in which you need to plan is your goal. The Bible says, "It is appointed unto man, once to die, and after that the judgment." Every one of us can reasonably expect either to die or to be raptured. The last time I checked, man's death rate was almost one hundred percent. A couple of people in the Bible escaped death, but that will not be true for most of us. We will die. Since that fact is established, why not take the time now to write your own epithet? What words do you want to be written on your tombstone? What do you want to be said about yourself? What do you want to have accomplished by the time you die? You need to write a statement as to what you want to be said on the day of your funeral. After you write that statement, you have to decide how you want to live your life to fulfill that statement. How do you want to impact people? How do you want to be remembered? Who do you want to be missed? Who do you want weeping at your funeral? Your mourners will only be those whose lives you touched, not those you robbed. Next, you need to write down what you want God to say to you when you get to heaven. When God greets you, what do you want Him to say to you? Do you want Him to say, "Well, you made it in?" Or, do you want to hear your Father say, "Well done, my child. You've served well; now come and reign well." That is what I want him to say about me. That's my goal, but it is not going to happen by accident. I have to develop a plan or a vision for accomplishing my goal, and so do you. If you want God to say, "Well done," you must "do well" while you are on this earth. Having a vision helps you measure how "well" you are doing.

THE TIMELINE: The second thing you have to do is develop a timeline. You may not know the exact date of your death, but you can turn to the Bible for a guideline regarding your life expectancy. The Bible promised us "three-score and ten" years (Psalms 90:10). That means the average person has a life expectancy of about seventy years. Some of us will live even longer than that, but let us use ninety as our gauge. Use that age to give you a timeline in your mind. Keeping that deadline in mind will help you realize that every day counts. Every day that you live is a day that you will not have again; every single second that goes by is a second that you will never see again. Using seventy as my own timeline means that, as of right now, I only have about 12,225 days of life left. That means if I waste tomorrow, I only have

12,224 days left to accomplish my destiny. In terms of your destiny, you need to see your own life in "numbered" days. You have a destiny and limited time to fulfill it. Take the time now to set your own timeline and count the days you have left to accomplish your vision. That will keep you on task.

A PLAN FOR SPIRITUAL GROWTH AND DEVELOPMENT

In order to stay on task, you must develop plans for certain areas of your life. I suggest the following areas for your initial focus:

1. Spiritual Plan
2. Family Plan
3. Service to God Plan
4. Career Plan
5. "Self" Plan
6. Leisure/Vacation Plan
7. Financial Plan
8. Health Plan

As you work through these plans, remember to float your plans through the lens of what you bring to the table. Your experience and your responses emotionally, mentally, etc. can help push your vision forward or need to be worked on during the process. Note these areas as well.

1. YOUR SPIRITUAL PLAN

If you are to grow in God, the first thing you should do is write your "vision statement." What do you want to do? Where do you want to go? You may say, "I want to be an anointed man (or woman) of God who loves God passionately." Whatever your spiritual desire is, write it down in a concise statement. That statement should be a sentence that says, "This is what I want to do; this is where I want to go."

Next, you must develop a plan to fulfill that statement. Write the details, not generalities. Be specific. For instance, a plan may have a specific time for prayer and Bible reading every day. Your plan may focus on scripture memorization; outlining the number of scriptures you will memorize every week. You may decide you are going to read the Bible every year, from cover to cover. You might plan to be in church every Sunday, if at all possible. You may decide to attend one conference per year or to read a certain number of books by the end of the year. Whatever your plan for your own spiritual development, you must write it down in an organized manner. Put down specific things that you are going to do and when you are going to do them so that you end up facilitating your plan for spiritual growth.

NOTES:

_____

_____

_____

_____

_____

_____

_____

_____

_____

_____

_____

_____

_____

_____

_____

_____

_____

_____

_____

_____

_____

_____

_____

_____

2. YOUR FAMILY PLAN

Your family plan should be just as plainly written as your spiritual plan. I once read a life plan that a husband wrote concerning his service to his wife. He wrote: "These are the things I'm going to do for my spouse: I'm going to pray every day for her. I'm going to be home by 6:00 pm each day. I will focus the first hour we're together on learning about her day. I'll date her one night per week. I'm going to be her best friend and spiritual leader." This man was very specific. If you are a wife, you can write a family plan that includes what you are going to do for your husband. Do not write, "I'm going to be a good wife." Be specific. You may write, "I'm going to massage him when he gets home from work. I'm going to build his self-esteem. I'm going to make his favorite casserole. I'm going to pray for him." Whatever you need to do, write it down, but you must be detailed and specific.

If you have children, they must also be part of your life plan. What are you going to do with your children? Don't just say, "I'm going to spend time with my children." Be specific. "I will take my kids to Fun Zone once a week, or to the park, or I'm going to let them decide where we go once a week. I'm going to read the Bible with them. I'm going to sit down and talk with them. I'm going to be available to them." Be specific with the things you are going to do. Do not leave your time with them to chance. Have a definite plan for your time together. Family development is a very important part of your own spiritual growth and development.

Appendix A: Developing a Life Plan

NOTES:

3. SERVICE-TO-GOD PLAN

You should even develop a plan for how you will serve God. Maybe you will grow from just planning to be "in" church to planning to plant a church that grows to ten thousand members. You may have a God-given vision of being an evangelist or a prophet. You may see yourself laying hands on the sick or casting devils out. You may want to be a solid layman, or you may want to witness to fifty people every year. Whatever your service plan is, be specific when writing it down. Do not leave it to happen by accident. Set goals for your plan. If you plan to witness for God, set a goal. You may desire to reach twenty-five, fifty, or even a hundred souls each year. Having a set goal causes you to make wise use of your time. You will take advantage of every available opportunity to witness because you are determined to achieve your goal. If you do not set specific goals, you may end up missing out on serious opportunities. How are you going to serve God? Write your own plan and be specific.

NOTES:

_____

_____

_____

_____

_____

_____

_____

_____

_____

_____

_____

_____

_____

_____

_____

_____

_____

_____

_____

_____

_____

_____

_____

_____

_____

4. CAREER PLAN

What kind of money are you going to make? What do you want to accomplish? What are your career goals? You need to write them down. You ought to be pressing for a promotion, not just pressing for a paycheck, which is probably not enough anyway. What are you doing at your job? Why are you there? Are you there in transition to another place? What are your goals? Please do not be at the mercy of your employer. Things are so uncertain that only God should be your source. Layoffs, cutbacks, and pink slips are issued on a regular basis. Do not put all your trust in your employer to dictate the quality of your life. Number one, God must be your source, and number two, you always need a backup plan. If you have a goal, you will not become as upset when unexpected events occur in your career. When your co-workers despair over getting pink slips, you have peace because you see the layoff as an opportunity to advance your goal. Little "bumps" on life's road do not discourage you because your vision causes you to look far beyond a temporary setback. Your focus is on where you are going, where your plan is taking you. That plan should include some kind of contingency for unexpected career "bumps" so that they do not become permanent roadblocks.

NOTES:

5. SELF-DEVELOPMENT PLAN

You also need to write your own self-development plan. How are you going to develop yourself to become better? Are you going to work on improving communication skills this year? Maybe you want to limit yourself to one hour of television per week. We should always try to develop ourselves. If you can sing well, that is a blessing; but do you want to develop into an even better singer? If you play an instrument, that is a blessing, but how much time do you need to devote to becoming an even more accomplished musician? You may have a natural gift for preaching and that is a blessing, but what specific steps do you need to take to develop your gift even more. Whatever you do, you can do better, but you have to develop a plan for self-improvement. How are you going to be a better student? You may want to start by improving your study habits. Write out a specific plan for your study times and your study environment. In whatever area you want to improve personally, write your plan with specific and achievable goals.

NOTES:

_____

_____

_____

_____

_____

_____

_____

_____

_____

_____

_____

_____

_____

_____

_____

_____

_____

_____

_____

_____

_____

_____

_____

_____

6. LEISURE/VACATION PLAN

I am beginning to understand the importance of fun and recreation. Just as God Himself rested on the seventh day, we must also have our "downtime." We need recreation. Those who have driven personalities must learn to slow down, or something will probably happen that will slow them down. We are not machines; we are men and women. We cannot continue to go and go and go. Even your car cannot run indefinitely without being serviced at some point. So how can you? We need downtime. We need fun time—a time of pure recreation that allows us to get away from the day-to-day pressures of life. There was a time in my life when I did not understand this truth. I had been serving God for more than fourteen years before I took a vacation. I never went away; I never did anything "fun." Even if I did get away, I withdrew for a season of fasting and praying, which meant that I came back even more tired because of denying the body. Finally, my church stepped in. One of the brothers collected an offering and sent my wife and me to Florida. During that vacation, I did not want to see a Bible, I did not want to see a church—I just got away. We went jet skiing and para-sailing. We just enjoyed our time together. We came back to our congregation refreshed and ready to serve. Downtime is critical. Every seven days, you should have a day of rest. Every month, you should take a couple of days off for pure relaxation if you can. The Bible calls it a recreation of the spirit. Downtime re-creates the spirit, re-creates the mind, and re-creates the body. If you do not take time to rest, you will become frustrated, and spiritually and naturally burned out. You will go from doing too much to doing nothing at all. When you find yourself about to give up on those things that you know

God has ordained you to do, check to see if you are suffering from spiritual burnout. If you are restless, just rest. Allow yourself to be refreshed and restored. You must plan that vacation or time of rest for yourself, otherwise you will allow it to be stolen from you.

NOTES:

_____

_____

_____

_____

_____

_____

_____

_____

_____

_____

_____

_____

_____

_____

_____

_____

_____

_____

_____

7. FINANCIAL PLAN

You need to plan your finances. You do not need to allow your income to come to you accidentally. Instead, you should have a goal for your earnings and a plan for reaching that goal. Then, work out your plan and believe God to make it happen. If you need outside help, find a reputable financial advisor. You should have your monthly budgetary items covered easily so that you can tithe and put money away for unexpected large expenses and vacations, as well as a retirement account. Put your earnings on a timetable and ask God to help you keep that schedule. And remember, vision produces action.

NOTES:

_____

_____

_____

_____

_____

_____

_____

_____

_____

_____

_____

_____

_____

_____

_____

_____

_____

_____

_____

_____

_____

_____

_____

_____

_____

8. HEALTH PLAN

You also need some goals related to your health. Maintaining a healthy lifestyle involves discipline and planning. If you want to correct a weight problem, you must find a weight-loss plan that fits you. Part of that plan must be a choice to discipline yourself in terms of your eating habits and food choices. Christians amaze me. Some are so undisciplined that they will sit and eat a banana split and pray, "God, curse these calories in this banana-split in Jesus' name." That kind of prayer will not work. Men cannot expect to eat fried chicken every day and not suffer the physical consequences. Your arteries will pop if you fill them up with cholesterol. Your pancreas will get tired when you bombard it with excessive amounts of sugar. It will say, "I am tired of producing all of this insulin, "I quit." That means you have to start injecting into your body the insulin you lack. It's called diabetes. High blood pressure will develop if you consistently eat the wrong things. For most of us, a lack of exercise increases our chances of contracting some health challenges, including heart disease and obesity. So, take care of yourself. Set goals that you can achieve. Eat more moderately and choose healthier foods. If you do not have an exercise routine, talk to your doctor and start one. You may start by just walking for fifteen to thirty minutes, three or four times a week. Whatever you decide to do, plan it. Do not just *talk* about changing or *dream* about a new you; make a plan with specific goals directed toward improving your health and maintaining a healthy lifestyle.

NOTES:

_____

_____

_____

_____

_____

_____

_____

_____

_____

_____

_____

_____

_____

_____

_____

_____

_____

_____

_____

_____

_____

_____

APPENDIX B

YOUR LIFE PLAN WORKSHEET

The Purpose Statement:

_____

_____

_____

_____

I will . . .

_____

_____

_____

_____

_____

_____

_____

_____

_____

The Goal:

   Who you want to be remembered by:

_____

_____

_____

   What you want to be remembered for:

_____

_____

_____

The Timeline:

_____

_____

_____

The Plans:

   Spiritual – I will...

_____

     Goals:

_____

_____

_____

   Family – I will...

_____

   Spouse – I will...

_____

Goals:

_____

_____

Children/Family – I will...

_____

Goals:

_____

_____

_____

Ministry – I will...

_____

Goals:

_____

_____

_____

Career – I will...

_____

Goals:

_____

_____

_____

Self-Development – I will...

_____

Goals:

_____

_____

Fun/Vacation – I will...

_____

    Goals:

_____

_____

Finance/My Dream – I will...

_____

    Goals:

_____

_____

Health – I will...

_____

    Goals:

_____

_____

_____

Appendix C
Sample Life Plan

The Purpose Statement:

I purpose to maximize my life for the glory of God and in pursuit of my full God-given potential.

I will . . .

- Strivw to live every day in such a manner that I sense God's pleasure in how I spent my day.

  (spiritual) _____

  _____

- Learn to love my wife as Christ loves the church.

  (marriage) _____

  _____

- Teach my children the ways of the Lord.

  (children/family) _____

  _____

- Make full proof of my ministry. 2 Tim 4:5

  (ministry) _____

  _____

- Give it my absolute best.

  (career) _____

  _____

- Never settle but commit daily to excellence.

  (self-development) _____

  _____

- Live, Love ,and Laugh daily.

  (fun/vacation) _____

  _____

- Trust God for Provision and labor according to Wisdom.

  (finance/Resources) _____

  _____

- Embrace stewardship of my body by taking care of it spiritually, mentally and emotionally.

  (health) _____

  _____

The Goal

Mark Johnson's Epitaph

1965 – 2065 *(100 years)*

"He Finished Well."

I want to be remembered, loved, and missed by:

- My wife and Family
- My Church Members
- Those I have ministered to

The Timeline

Live a total of 100 years (2065) As of 2/28/2022 . . . 15,695 Days remaining! *(43 years).*

The Plan

_____

_____

_____

_____

_____

_____

_____

_____

_____

_____

_____

_____

_____

_____

_____

Spiritual

·   Seek to live every day in such a manner that I sense God's pleasure over the way I spent my day./ Strive to live every day in such a way that I can sense God's pleasure in how I spent my day.

1. Spend a minimum of one hour per day alone with God in prayer.
2. Memorize one Bible verse each week.
3. Read through the Bible each year.
4. Read the following books by the end of 2022:
   a. January—*Crazy Love*, by Francis Chan
   b. February—*The Spiritual Man*, Watchman Nee
   c. March—*The Celebration of Discipline*, by Richard Foster
   d. April—*The Purpose Driven Life*, by Rick Warren
   e. May—*Insurgence*, by Frank Viola
   f. June—*Solitude*, by Michael Harris
   g. July—*Encounters with Jesus*, by Timothy Keller
   h. August—*Emotionally Healthy Spirituality*, by Peter Scazzaro
   i. September—*Humility*, by Andrew Murray
   j. October—*Strength to Love*, by Martin Luther King Jr.
5. Keep a journal of what God shows me.
6. Seek regularly to experience present tense God encounters.

Spouse

· Learn to love my wife as Christ loves the church.

1. Pray daily for Jemimah's needs.

2. Have a date night once per week (dinner and talking).

3. One weekend away every quarter.

4. End each day with prayer.

5. Be her friend, dwell with her according to knowledge

Children/Family

· Teach my children the ways of the Lord.

1. Pray daily for my children and grandchildren .

2. Play Bible trivia games

3. Teach them to have a devotional life.

4. Read one book on parenting each year.

5. Each year, put $1,000 in a college fund.

6. Each year, put $1,000 in a Roth IRA for each child.

7. Travel with my children individually when I go for ministry

Ministry

· Make full proof of my ministry, 2 Tim 4:5.

1. Pray daily for clarity of vision and direction for ministry.

2. Grow my church to:

   § 3000 membership

   § 200 small groups

   § 50 paid staff

§ 24 hours a day prayer

§ Plant 30 churches

§ Minister in 50 nations of the world.

§ Demonstrate signs and wonders in ministry.

§ Lead people to be worshippers of God and be a deliverer of men by my efforts.

§ Give millions of dollars away to the Kingdom.

§ See hundreds saved each year.

I will do this by:

a. Fervent Prayer and Fasting.

b. Studying and practicing the principles of church growth.

c. Raising and training leaders.

d. Following the plan, vision, and timing of God for my ministry.

e. Seek to be mentored by other giants in the faith.

f. Pray some more.

Career

Give it my absolute best.

1. Grow XYZ Company to a $XX-million-dollar company by 2025 with an XX% net profit margin.

2. Grow XYZ Company revenues to $XX million by 2026 while maintaining an XX% Marketing COGS.

3. Establish me as a qualified and capable CEO by 2026.

Self-Development

I WILL . . . Never settle but commit daily to excellence.

1. Attend one conference each year for professional growth.
2. Attend one conference each year for ministry growth.
3. Limit TV to no more than one hour each day/night.
4. Read two biographies each year
   a. Elon Musk (2022)
   b. Colin Powell (2023)

Fun/Vacation

· I WILL Live, Love, and Laugh daily.

1. Each year. take three weeks of vacation with my wife.
2. Get API rating by Dec 2025.
3. Visit Dubai.
4. Vacation in Hawaii.
5. Give my wife a surprise vacation once every three years.

Finance/My Dream

I WILL . . . Trust God for Provision and labor according to wisdom.

1. Give XX% of my gross income to tithe (2023).
3. Give XX% of my gross income to tithe (2025).
4. Give XX% of my gross income to tithe (2026).
5. Give XX% of my gross income to tithe (2027).
6. Give XX% of my gross income to tithe (2028).

7. Give XX% of my gross income to tithe (2029).

8. Purchase one investment property every other.

9. Flip one investment property each year.

10. Increase my financial IQ by the following:

    · Spend 30 minutes each night reading (3.5 hrs/wk).

    · Attend an Entrepreneurial Seminar each year.

    · Have a wealthy person mentor me.

Health

I WILL . . . Embrace stewardship of my body by taking care of it spiritually, mentally, and emotionally.

1. Reach 225 lbs by 6/25/2022 and maintain it with a 38-inch waist.

2. Work out three times each week.

3. Workout two additional days for supplemental cardio (jump rope).

4. Continue eating a Whole Foods Plant-Based Diet until 225 lbs is achieved.

5. Drink 125 oz of water each day.

6. Go to bed at 10:00 pm (read for one hour) and get up at 7 am.

ENDNOTES

Chapter 1

1 https://en.wikipedia.org

ABOUT KYLE

Pastor

Kyle Searcy is the senior pastor of Fresh Anointing House of Worship, a 2,000-member church located in Montgomery, Alabama. He also serves as presiding Bishop of the Fresh Oil Fellowship of churches and nine Fresh Anointing House of Worship churches in the United States.

Kyle's love for God and people is reflected in his evangelistic and humanitarian efforts nationwide and abroad. His passion for youth and young adults here in America led him to form Youth City. This organization provides a holistic approach to meeting the needs of at-risk youth and young people (Generation Z and Millennials.) Additionally, he oversees 130 international churches throughout the continent of Africa in countries such as Liberia, Nigeria, and Ghana.

Leader

Kyle's passion for developing a new generation of Christ-centered and community-centric leaders led him to become the KCS Leadership Institute founder. He uses his leadership capacity to diligently serve in various key roles at the local, state, national, and international levels. Kyle is a sought-after speaker and conducts leadership summits, seminars, and conferences worldwide.

Author

Family Man

Kyle is husband to his beautiful wife Kemi for 31 years. They are the blessed parents of four beautiful children and six grandchildren. The happy couple enjoy reading and doing puzzles in their spare time. As a licensed pilot for over 17 years, Kyle and Kemi also enjoy traveling through the friendly skies and taking road trips together.

Contact

Email: kylesearcy@fahow.org

Call: 334-613-3363

Or www.kylesearcy.com

Online Services

www.fahow.org

www.youtube.com/freshanointing

Facebook: Fresh Anointing House of Worship

Mission School in Sierra Leone

To learn about or help sponsor a student in our school in Sierra Leone, visit

www.DestinyChristianAcademyAfrica.com